Full Circle

Full Circle

A New Look at Multiage Education

Penelle Chase and Jane Doan

HEINEMANN
Portsmouth, NH

Heinemann
A division of Reed Elsevier Inc.
361 Hanover Street
Portsmouth, NH 03801–3912
Offices and agents throughout the world

Every effort has been made to contact the copyright holders and students for permission to reprint borrowed material. We regret any oversights that may have occurred and would be happy to rectify them in future printings of this work.

Chapter 10, "From Multiage to Multiple Ways of Knowing: Discovering the Strengths of Our Children" by Jean Anne Clyde contains a condensed version of a portion of the article "Lessons from Douglas: Expanding Our Visions of What It Means to Know" by Jean Anne Clyde (*Language Arts,* Vol. 71, January 1994).

Editors: Philippa Stratton and Dawn Boyer
Production: Renée M. Pinard
Text Design: Jenny Jensen Greenleaf
Cover Design: Darci Mehall

Library of Congress Cataloging-in-Publication Data

Chase, Penelle.
    Full circle : a new look at multiage education / Penelle Chase and Jane Doan.
       p.   cm.
    Includes bibliographical references
     ISBN 0–435–08814–9
     1. Nongraded schools.   I. Doan, Jane.   II. Title.
LB1029.N6C47 1994
371.2'54—dc20   94–2168
                                        CIP

Printed in the United States of America on acid-free paper
99 98 97 96 95 94 EB 1 2 3 4 5 6

This book is for

Addison and Bob

Contents

Part Three: The Research Sphere

Preface

Penny's Journal: September 28

Today I worked with some children in the submarine. It was truly a multiaged group. Tanya, Jacob, and Benny are five. Lewis and Carter are six. Leslie, Heidi, and Chester are seven. What an exciting crew! They kept busy all during our Investigations Workshop time, and many of them wanted to come back to work in the sub again later at Choice Time. Eric and Hollis joined us then, too. Lewis made a periscope out of a paper towel tube. We suspended it from the ceiling with yarn. Chester made a hand-held telephone which he hung from the wall, with directions written next to it, describing how you contact land. Tanya made a whale with black and white paper, very detailed, to put in the waters outside. Jacob worked seriously with markers and large paper on an elaborate control panel. Carter did the air supply—he wrote *ON* and *OFF* on one set of controls, and he experimented with numbers telling us that the submarine was down this deep: 151511. Chester named the sub, *The Sinker and Finder*—it's a research sub, and Heidi made name signs for both the doors. The group really got into the spirit of outfitting the sub to do underwater experiments. Heidi made a collecting basket and Eric made a remote control arm. The children helped each other amiably—tearing tape, supplying scissors, etc. They were so involved, talking together to explain what their creations could do. Their talk seemed to actually generate new inspirations. They all contributed, accepting and building on each others' ideas. Lewis was in his element: "We're helping to make research!" Everyone experienced success. What else do we need in school?

Our multiaged classroom is a rich environment. It is rich in activity. It is rich in sociability. It is rich in differences. The talk here is energetic. Ideas ripple through the room. Caring happens naturally. We believe that learning in a multiaged setting is the happiest way to learn.

We are in our fifth year of co-teaching a multiaged group of five-, six-, seven-, and eight-year-olds. Each June we regretfully bid farewell to only those children who "graduate" from our program to enter third grade. Thankfully, we are secure in the knowledge that two-thirds of our class will return as old friends in the fall. We know, too, that the multiage cycle will continue then as we welcome the new youngest members of the class. Our multiage program keeps going on its own. It is a happy way to teach.

Many educators have visited us in our multiage classroom. They are realizing that this way of grouping children makes sense theoretically. Now they are eagerly seeking practical information. How can multiage education operate in real life? They have come to find out how we do it. They watch, they interact with the children, they pick our brains at recess time and after school. Most of them go away with a clearer view of how they will create a multiage environment that works for them.

It is our belief that each community and each school has its own unique needs that must be addressed by those involved in school restructuring. We know there is a great demand for information that can help educators to formulate their thoughts on multiage education, so that they can develop programs that will work for them. The intent of this book is to share our ideas.

The book is divided into three parts. In the first part, *Circles*, we note the historical roots of the multiage movement and describe our personal endeavors in multiage education.

In Chapter One, "Circling Back," we discuss the resurgence of interest in the multiage movement and explore reasons for this renewed interest. We also include a brief history of our teaching careers to show how we have come to believe that multiage education offers the best possible learning forum for children and adults alike.

Chapter Two, "One Day," explores a day in our classrooms. In describing our beginning of the day circle and the end of the day circle we explain the function of talk in our program. We discuss the process of our Morning Message, in which we set the tone of the day, teach reading and spelling strategies, and demonstrate the mechanics of written language. The bulk of the chapter is a description of our workshop format, through which we integrate learning across the curriculum and meet the varied needs of our students. We show how Choice Time, Communications Workshop, Investigations Workshop, and Math Workshop provide opportunities for us all to engage in purposeful learnings. Finally, we describe how other adults enrich our program.

Chapter Three is called "Our Views." In this chapter we discuss our personal beliefs. Our thoughts on co-teaching and how we practice it are a major focus. We also discuss aspects that we feel are most important to the success of a multiage program:

- a community of learners
- real learning for real reasons
- themes, student choice, and responsibility
- a family environment
- a workshop format
- parent involvement.

In Chapter Four, "Valuing," we discuss how our students show us what they value, and how we show the parents what we value about their children. We describe how the students set goals and how they have created portfolios. We discuss our methods of teacher observation, our class record books, and our formal parent conferences, as well as our progress report. We show how co-teaching helps us to value our students.

Chapter Five, "The Little Room," tells about the evolution of the dramatic play area in our classrooms. We discuss the value of dramatic play in a multiage setting, how groupings are set up, and how the students become self-directed through their play. Finally, we describe examples of some of the theme-related activities and experiences that have occurred in the Little Room.

We use Chapter Six, "The Pumpkin Project," to describe in detail our pumpkin growing and marketing enterprise. We show how the pumpkin project has all the essential elements for meaningful education, illustrating how important it has become in our multiage setting. We show how this project allows for the integration of learning from every subject area and how it provides real work for real reasons. This ongoing project is the absolute coming together of our ideas on multiage learning.

The second part, *Ripples*, is a medley of writings by other multiage educators. Their varied experiences give the reader a broader understanding of the multiage movement and of the diverse applications of multiage grouping.

Chapter Seven, "Widening Circles," is a collection of "snippets" written by a variety of multiage educators from across the United States. Their writings address many of the specific questions being asked about the practicalities of designing and implementing multiage programs.

In Chapter Eight, "Multiage: A Parent's View," Katy Alioto, whose two children have been in our program, gives a parent's perspective of the benefits of a multiage environment.

Kathy McDonough and Katie Johnson in Chapter Nine, "Safe and Successful: Emotionally Disturbed Children in the Multiage Setting," describe how a multiage structure benefits the children at Knight Children's Center in Massachusetts.

In Chapter Ten, "From Multiage to Multiple Ways of Knowing: Discovering the Strengths of Our Children," Jean Anne Clyde discusses the results of her research in a primary multiage class in Kentucky.

Gary MacDonald in Chapter Eleven, "Creating and Sustaining a Multiage Vision," tells how he and the teachers in a small rural school in Maine restructured from traditional to multiage classes.

The third part, *The Research Sphere*, presents an extensive review of the literature on multiage grouping. Diane E. McClellan is the author of this final chapter, "Multiage Grouping: Implications for Education."

The appendices include our checklist for observing Morning Message, a sample parent newsletter, our parent survey, our student goal-setting sheet, our parent conference sheet, a list of suggested end-of-day questions, and our progress report.

As multiage educators, we welcome you to share your comments and questions with us. Please send correspondence to the authors and contributors in care of Heinemann (see address on page iv).

Acknowledgments

We would like to thank our friend and teacher, Brenda Power. Her insistence and support convinced us that we could indeed write this book.

Our children, Phoebe and Meg, Michael and Kathryn, have been our best teachers. We treasure their enthusiastic support of our work as educators and writers.

To all those who raised us and who are still influencing our lives, we owe our love of reading and writing. Thank you.

We thank the contributors to this book. Their ideas broaden our concept of multiage education.

We are grateful to Dr. Edward Fabian, Superintendent of Schools in School Administrative District #49, who listened to our ideas and encouraged us to "go for it!" We appreciate the principals of Benton Elementary, Suanne Giorgetti and John Bacon, whose trust and confidence supported us as we developed our multiage program.

Finally, we thank the children in our multiage classes and their parents. Without them there would not have been this story.

Part One:
Circles

Circling Back

1

Jane Doan

The children are full of anticipation. They have been waiting all year for this trip back in time to the Norlands School of 1853. They even raised the money to pay for the trip by selling pumpkins the previous fall. Their recent study of "Life Long Ago" has created an intense interest in what school was like for children in the 1850s. Curiosity and excitement show on every face as the bus pulls into the barnyard of the Norlands Living History Museum near Livermore Falls, Maine. The small wooden schoolhouse down the road from the restored farmhouse is to be the site of our participation in the reenactment of an old-fashioned school day. Many of the children have come today dressed in period clothing. They eagerly gather around Mrs. Howard, the schoolmarm, as she explains how they must "make their manners" to her before they enter her schoolhouse. The old-fashioned terms intrigue them. When they are asked to line up in two lines, a girls' and a boys' line, they are ready and even line up according to age. I am amazed at the quiet. "Penny, have you ever heard such silence?" I softly ask my co-teacher. Inside, the scholars sit up straight at the wooden desks and listen patiently and carefully as the day's tasks are announced. Each child is given a task that suits his or her abilities and needs.

"I like this school," whispers six-year-old Joanna as she works at writing her name with a quill pen. "I like going to school in 1853," she continues. I have to agree with her, but I wonder if Joanna likes this old-fashioned school because of the similarities to her own school situation, rather than the differences. Like the class of 1853, Joanna's class is a mix of children of many ages. In her class the children's ages range from five to eight years. Like the children in the school of 1853, Joanna's classmates are encouraged and expected to help one another. Cooperative learning, collaboration, and peer teaching are the norm. Like the class of 1853, Joanna's class will encounter the same teachers for a number of years who will follow the students' growth as they progress individually through the curriculum. Like the children in the school of

1853, Joanna's class shares a "family experience." Like the children of 1853, Joanna is a member of a multiage class.

A National Movement

The multiage concept is undergoing a resurgence in popularity in the 1990s. All over the United States schools are restructuring to multiage programs. Some states, like Kentucky and Oregon, have mandated multiage programs for their primary classrooms. Others, like Maine, have strongly supported movement toward multiage education through innovative grants and state workshops.

This renewed interest in the multiage philosophy may be an outgrowth of the progressive movement in education. Patrick Shannon (1990) writes of the history of this movement, which began in the seventeenth century with the teachings of Comenius. Comenius argued for a developmental view of education and maintained that children would need less discipline if the curriculum made sense to them. In *The Struggle to Continue*, Shannon tells us that "Comenius suggested multiage groupings so that 'one pupil serves as an example and a stimulus for another'" (22). Shannon also documents the ideals and histories of progressive schools based on the multiage concept, which works for children and adults alike. Among the progressive schools he describes are the Quincy Schools of the 1870s, in which individuality was the system; the Moonlight Schools in Kentucky, where students served as instructors under the slogan, "Each one teach one"; and the Highlander Folk School in Tennessee, where staff members were instructed to teach by demonstrating their capacity to learn.

The multiage concept is receiving renewed attention because it allows educators to move toward a more developmentally appropriate educational program. It offers a reasonable solution to problems inherent in the outmoded practices of ability tracking and grade retention. The developmental philosophy encourages educators to address individual differences in children. As teachers recognize individual differences, they realize that there is no graded curriculum appropriate for all students of a particular age. In a multiage classroom children of differing ages work together, with each child participating to the best of his or her abilities. Since children remain in multiage classes for more than one year, their growth and learning is individually paced.

Multiage classrooms also provide a natural extension to the whole language approach to literacy and the problem solving approach to math. These movements encourage student use of literacy and math for real purposes. Since it is common for curriculum to drive the learning in graded classrooms, it can be difficult for students to experience language and math in authentic contexts. In multiage classrooms teachers find that the wide variety of ability levels facilitates the promotion of choice and the students' ownership of learning. Ownership leads to learning for real reasons. The children readily become readers, writers, and mathematicians for their own purposes. They see reasons for the work they are doing, due to the individual nature of that work in the multiage setting.

Children in multiage programs are supported as learners. The emphasis is on what each child *can* do. Assessment strategies such as "kidwatching," portfolios, exhibitions, and checklists are used to evaluate student progress, rather than standardized tests. Teacher knowledge of each student is enhanced in a multiage program through these natural forms of assessment. The ability to watch a child's progress over a period of several years also gives teachers a unique opportunity to know their students.

Children are supported socially in multiage groupings, as well. A family environment in which children are expected to assume responsibility for themselves and for their peers is the cornerstone of the multiage philosophy. In such a setting children develop lasting relationships with each other and with their teachers. Community values evolve through caring about "family" members.

The distinguished history of the multiage concept is prompting today's educators to take a new look at this effective educational practice. Current trends in education support multiage grouping as a valid environment for social maturation, for emotional stability, and for academic learning. The multiage movement has returned with renewed energy. We are proud to be a part of it.

Becoming Multiage Educators

A history of our teaching careers shows how we came to the conclusion that multiage teaching was for us. We began our multiage program in 1988. Our decision to start this program was the result of our individual teaching experiences and of our many years of questioning our teaching practices. Our reasons for moving in this direction, while personal to a great extent, are also similar to the reasons that teachers all over the nation are embracing this movement.

In 1972 I returned to teaching in Waterville, Maine, after spending five years at home parenting my two children. Prior to the birth of my son, I had taught a first-grade class in Pennsylvania; at that time I was a very traditional teacher. My students sat in rows. I had three reading groups. I lectured and expected the children to grasp what I said. If they didn't learn my curriculum, I considered them to be failures. When I applied for a teaching position at the South Grammar School in Waterville I was definitely from the old school of teaching. However, as a parent of two young children, I was beginning to question my educational philosophy. I was learning a lot from my children about teaching that had not been a part of the curriculum at West Chester State Teacher's College! I was beginning to believe that teachers must teach children first, before focusing on the curriculum. I was hired, probably because of what my children had taught me.

At this time Penny was beginning her third year as a teacher. She had graduated from college with a Liberal Arts degree in English Literature. Her first teaching experience had been in a school district where basal readers were required for the teaching of reading. During that year she took a course from the University of Maine called "Newer Practices in Teaching Reading." In this course she was exposed to the idea of using an individualized reading program and wished to use this method in her classroom. In order to teach in the style she felt was best, Penny moved to the South Grammar school in Waterville, where Individualized Reading programs were the norm. When I was hired she was in her second year there, a year that was to bring many changes to the way all the teachers in that school perceived the educational process.

Our experiences together at South Grammar School that year were our first steps toward becoming co-teachers in a multiage program. There we began to look at our teaching in a reflective way. The school was in the process of restructuring from traditional to multi-graded classrooms. Five one/two combinations and four three/four combination classrooms, as well as a kindergarten, made up the ten-classroom school. Penny taught one of the three/four classrooms and I was in charge of a one/two grouping. The children were to stay with the same teacher for two years.

The best part of this restructuring was that teachers were encouraged to share ideas. We even had common planning time built into our schedule to do this sharing. On Thursdays each week the children were dismissed early and the staff held an inservice from 2:00 to 4:00. The entire school studied the same themes and shared information learned through assemblies and cross-grade groupings.

We were guided through this unique restructuring experience by two gifted educators who were to become our role models. Dr. Dorothy Raymond, Director of Reading, and Caroline Sturtevant, Title I Supervisor, developed the plan to effect changes at our school, which was located in the low income section of the central Maine city of Waterville. Their progressive thinking influenced us greatly.

During the first year we experienced the intense high of being a part of an exciting new program. We also often experienced the intense low of being confused and unsure of the direction we were taking. The second year we felt more secure as we began to reap the benefits of having a class that consisted of many students who had been with us the year before. These children quickly initiated the younger students into the rites of our particular classrooms. We did not need to use the first few weeks of school to disseminate facts about class rules and procedures. Half of the class was already a cohesive group, and they made sure that the new children quickly became a part of our family.

Through this teaching experience we first saw the benefits of family grouping. We discovered that being together as a group for an extended period of time gave children the opportunity to develop meaningful relationships with others. Students developed the confidence that allowed them to take risks as learners. We learned that a mixed-age class acquires a shared sense of purpose, an aura of caring that does not seem apparent in traditional single-grade classes, especially in those large schools where the children are mixed and matched each year. We learned that when the class consisted of children of many ages it was easy to move away from ability grouping and grade retention. It was possible to move away from lecturing and memorizing towards challenging the children to become thinkers. We adopted an individualized program that concentrated more on each child's needs, rather than on a prescribed curriculum.

The Waterville experiment lasted four years. At the end of that time, the school board decided that all the district's schools must be the same and therefore our program must stop. With funding growing tight, the district was not willing to finance experimental programs. We were forced to restructure to traditional classes. Penny took a leave from teaching to have her children, and I went to teach at a small private school. A year later the district was reorganized and our school was closed. The experiment was over. But for Penny and me, inquiry into our teaching was just beginning.

Four years later Penny and I were reunited in another school district in Maine, which included the towns of Albion, Benton, Clinton, and Fairfield. Penny taught in the small rural K-6 Albion school, and I taught at a primary school in the larger town of Fairfield. Penny taught a combined first- and second-grade class created as a necessity due to the number of students at those levels. This district used basals, but Penny was eager to move toward a more child-centered approach to teaching literacy. She successfully replaced basals with a literature-based program. She spent eight years teaching combined classes, building on her valuable experiences at the South Grammar School in Waterville. At my school in Fairfield I also was assigned to a combined first- and second-grade class, and I kept the entire class again the next year as second and third graders. Basals disappeared from my shelves, too, as I realized that in such a classroom individualized instruction was a necessity. Following this experience I was assigned to teach a pre-first class of children who were deemed not developmentally ready for first grade. During this period I made the greatest changes in my teaching style, working toward a child-centered curriculum.

Though we taught in different schools, Penny and I began to see a lot of each other as we worked toward our Masters degrees in Education at the University of Maine. We took courses together in order to carpool and to make the long commute more pleasant. In one of our courses we co-authored a paper on multiage classes, and we made the decision to work toward starting a true multiage program in our district. Our reasons for this decision were personal as well as philosophical.

My primary concern was parent choice. As a teacher in the school district where my children attended school, I had been able to select their teachers. I believe that this privilege is one that all parents should have. I also believe that parents should have a choice of educational programs for their children. When parents are able to have some control of their children's education, they become true partners in educating their child. When the parents are welcomed as participants in the educational process, this partnership leads to a well-defined family connection to the classroom.

I wanted to return to teaching in a family environment in which children are grouped with others of various ages. I knew that segregating children by age was artificial and had little academic benefit. In a multiage setting children naturally learn from each other. Individual differences are respected and children are allowed and encouraged to learn at their own rates.

Penny's main incentive for wanting to move to a multiage program was her desire to allow children time to grow and learn without the label of failure. She was distressed each January when she met with parents (as part of our district's requirements) to discuss possible retention of children who were not on "grade level." She knew that retention does not help children. Her classroom experience indicated that there was another way. One year when she was discussing the possibility of retention with a parent of a first-grade student in her one/two combination class, the parent suggested that Penny just keep the child in her class another year and not label him as being "kept back." If the child was not reading and writing successfully by the end of the next year, they could discuss retention then. In the meantime they would just allow the child a year's time to grow and learn in a supportive environment. By the next January, there was no longer any concern about the child's academic progress. Time had done the trick!

Many schools in central Maine have so-called combination classes. The small rural schools often have grade-level groupings of a size too large for one classroom and too small to warrant the expense of hiring two teachers. Historically, the goal of these schools has been to eliminate these combined grades in favor of the more standard single-grade-level classrooms. Penny found, though, that many parents requested that their children remain with her for the two-year span. She did not run her class as a "combination class," teaching the first-grade students and then giving them busy work while she taught the second-grade children. Instead, she individualized her program and ran a workshop type class. She found that she enjoyed the opportunity to have two years to work with the students. In this span of time she was able to learn each child's strengths and needs. She could provide the children with developmentally appropriate learning situations. The success of her "combination classes" convinced her of the need to make this kind of teaching situation a standard in our district.

We took our multiage paper from our course at the University of Maine to our superintendent. We asked him to read it and to allow us to develop a multiage program of our own. Our timing was perfect! The district was building a new, very large, elementary school. Dr. Edward Fabian was interested in offering parents educational choices at this new building, and our proposal gave him the chance to do just that. He approved our plan and sent us to the school board with our request. They approved the plan, perhaps because they, too, saw the possibilities for educational change in the new school.

We began our multiage program in the fall of 1988. While the new school was being built, our first year was spent in a wonderful old school building where we co-taught using large classrooms located across the hall from each other. These rooms were separated from the rest of the school by the administrative offices and the girls' bathroom. We were alone together at the end of a long corridor. This isolation helped us to initiate our program in a relaxed manner. During that first year we began to explore how we could work together as co-teachers. But more important, we began to discover more about how children could learn in a multiage setting.

We have spent the last four years in a new school in connecting classrooms. During these years we have continued to look at the whys of what we are doing, to question our beliefs, and to refine our philosophy. We have also surveyed our parents and students to find out what is working or not working for them. In this way we have fine-tuned our program. The next five chapters describe our efforts so far, but we know our program will keep changing as we continue to learn from our students and their parents.

References

SHANNON, PATRICK. 1990. *The Struggle to Continue: Progressive Reading Instruction in the United States.* Portsmouth, NH: Heinemann.

One Day

2

Penelle Chase

8:00 A.M.

It's Monday morning, before school, January 25. I am pawing through the art shelves in my classroom. "I can't find that package of paper bags we're going to need for mammal puppets!" I yell to Jane. "I think you put them in your closet," she yells back from her room. Some buses have started to arrive, and children are drifting into the large common area outside our classrooms. Jane is out there now. I hear her greeting children, "Good morning, Gregory. Hi, Rebecca. Carter, you got a haircut! Didn't your ears get cold? Oh, you were wearing your hat. Good! Stuff it into your sleeve, so it doesn't get lost. Whose homework is that on the floor? It's getting stepped on. It needs to go into the homework basket!"

Head in the closet, I hear Barry and Benny coming through the door, having their usual discussion. "I'm the first one in the room!" "No, I am!"

"Good morning, boys!" I say, still digging. Aha! There they are! As I stretch to reach the bags in the back corner of the closet, I sense a whirlwind behind me, and I am grabbed around the knees in a tight hug. "Hi, Penny! I'm staying all day today!" It's Tara, of course, still in her jacket and snow pants, smelling of cold air. I turn in the circle of her arms and smile down at her, "Yes! Isn't it exciting?"

She nods vigorously. "I even brought my lunch!" I can pick out Tara's trail into the room, mittens, book bag, lunch box strewn at intervals from the door.

"Go take care of your stuff, you rascal!" My voice is as stern as I can muster. "Fast! So you can sign up for Choice Time."

She's off, gathering her belongings, snagging Darcy on her way by: "Will you read me the choices, Darcy?"

Of course Darcy will oblige. There is a group of children by the chart stand, studying the offerings for the Choice Time that will happen soon.

11

Others are taking their clothespins off the attendance card to show that they are here. Some have signed up at the board to do jobs. Krista chose to put out the snack. She has emptied two packages of saltines into the plastic bag in the snack basket. Now she is working on a sign: "You cn hav 4." Eric has gone into Jane's room to illustrate one of the poems we will read from the charts later at message time. Hollis has signed his name next to Post-its on the job sign-up list. I see him looking lost. "Dan, will you show Hollis how to put the Post-its in the class record books? He's never done it before." Some children are beginning to gather on the rug, getting ready for Talking Journal. Tracy is impressing a little crowd there with his new Batman figure. Susan and Benny are sitting with their heads close together. I hear Susan counseling him, "In the lunchroom when the lights go off, it's time to be quiet. When they go on you can talk." Benny nods.

Last Friday's session with the older children has paid off, I think to myself. Everyone had been looking forward to the first-year students staying all day, and we had done some brainstorming on Friday afternoon about how we could help them feel comfortable. Until today, our youngest children had gone home before lunch. Now they would stay all day on Mondays. As the weeks went by, we would add Fridays, then Wednesdays as possible whole days, too, depending on the needs of the first-year children and the wishes of their parents. During the last few weeks of school most of the children would probably be coming all day, every day. Today, though, is a landmark day, and I am hearing many references to "staying all day" in the children's chatter this morning. Once again I am thankful that we have the big kids to help them out. Susan's concern for Benny is typical in our class. Just as Darcy eagerly helped others read the Choice Time list, just as Dan willingly agreed to help Hollis with the Post-its, the other older children take their responsibilities toward the younger class members seriously.

We refer to this fifteen minute before-the-bell time as Visiting Time. It has become one of the most important times of our day. When children arrive at school they can choose to play outdoors or to come into the classroom. Most like to come right inside. After hanging up their coats, taking their name clips off the attendance card, and putting their homework papers in the basket, children are free to talk with friends and just "hang out." Jane and I hang out, too. We cherish this easy-going, relaxed time to greet the children and chat with them individually.

8:20 A.M.

Our formal day starts with the bell, the signal to make our circle on the rug for Talking Journal. Our circles at the beginning and end of the day include only the children on our own class lists. At other times during the day the kids mix between the two rooms. At the bell two of Jane's kids, Gregory and Leslie, scurry to her room. A few of mine return from her room, quickly finish their before-school responsibilities, and grab what they have brought to share with the group. Chester comes in late and Kristen pounces on him. Their names are on the board for filling out the attendance slip; she has been waiting impatiently for her day to come up again. Chester will probably let her do the writing today, but he'll be there if she needs help. Our circle is forming. "Scooch back, so everyone can fit," I remind them. "Who will start today?"

Tanya shows and tells us about her little statue of a horse. Zack announces that his mother is sick today. Serene shares her knowledge of impending meteor showers, which her family has been reading about in the paper. Hollis displays a radiator hose and tells about the car trouble that happened when he and his dad were on their way home yesterday. Almost all the children's stories are about their families or about special objects brought from home. We listen to each other. We comment, exclaim, and question. It is a comfortable way to ease into the school day.

8:45 A.M.

Choice Time is next. I take the Choice Time sign-up sheet from the chart stand. We pass through the little room that connects our two classrooms and all gather in Jane's room to compare charts and see who has chosen what. The children are on the rug; Jane is at her chart stand directing traffic. I greet Chester's mom, who is here to help at the woodworking bench, "I am glad that Jane is such a good organizer; at times like these I just want to throw my hands up in the air and run!"

The choices are varied. Many choices, like blocks, Legos, reading, writing, painting, plays, and games are standard fare every Choice Time. Others change each day. We write all of the choice offerings for the day on the two Choice Time sign-up charts, leaving numbered spaces below each choice. Children have written their names by the numbers to indicate their choices. We have new wooden blocks which we bought, along with some big cardboard bricks, with some of the money we earned selling pumpkins last fall. To be sure that everyone gets a turn to play with these new toys, we have signed up a group under *Blocks*. The current theme under study is mammals, so *Mammal Puppets with Penny* is on the list this morning. *Assembling Bricks with Jane* is there, too. The forty-eight cardboard bricks were delivered in a flat state two weeks ago, and it took us that long to figure out that the children were perfectly capable of helping us put them together. We find that we have to constantly remind ourselves of how much children can do. Allowing them to *do* is one way to give them ownership of their classroom.

After the initial hubbub, Jane gets everyone going in the right directions. Great things begin to happen. Thomas and Miranda take the big pillows out to the common area to read in quiet and comfort. Though Thomas is heavily involved in research about energy during Communications Workshop, he is enthusiastic about reading aloud to younger children like Miranda at Choice Time. Lewis, Justin, Lisbet, and Dan settle down with calculators and the Yahtzee game. The older ones will teach Dan the game today, and he will learn to use the calculator, too, as he adds up his score. Gregory, Roger, and Darcy are searching for a little book that would make a good play. They have already elaborately costumed themselves with articles from the dress-ups chest. They seem unconcerned that they have put the cart before the horse. Nan and Zack are organizing the new bricks on the shelves. In spite of exclamations like "Oh no, here come some more!" they enthusiastically redesign their storage scheme with each new load of bricks delivered by one of the crew working with Jane in her room. A group of four is with me at the big table. We're using scraps from the scrap box to make details on our bag mammal puppets. Mine is an elephant, Tracy's is a zebra, Tanya's is a horse, and Eric is making a bat. We're all pretty proud of our creations so far. "When we share these after Choice Time maybe we could have the animals tell something about themselves," Tracy suggests. "Good idea!" we agree, and I move to turn off the lights for quiet. My five-minute warning before clean-up time is greeted with groans. I'm sad, too. The last forty minutes have been energetic and purposeful. So much learning happens when we give kids the freedom to make discoveries, to dabble, to talk, to relax, to cooperate, and to create. We need to keep searching out more ways like this to allow them to learn on their own.

Clean-up accomplished, we sit together again in the large open space in Jane's room for a quick sharing of the mammal puppets, a mural Leslie and Hannah worked on in Jane's room, and the play, which miraculously came together during the last five minutes of Choice Time. Now it is time for Morning Message.

9:30 A.M.

Jane will lead the message today, and I will be an observer. I sit at a table off to the side of the group. With me I have a supply of Post-its and the message checklist (see Appendix A). I will focus particularly hard on the seven children whose names are on this checklist. On the Post-its,

I will note significant comments, questions, and discoveries that other children make, as well. Today it is Lewis's turn to be the student observer. He sits near me with his own supply of Post-its. During warm-up, I watch him scanning the children as together they read the poem hanging on the chart stand. It is about a leopard in the zoo. Lewis writes on one Post-it, "Darcy red with good espreshin." After reading the poem, Jane asks the children how they think the leopard feels to be in a cage. They talk a few minutes about whether or not we should have zoos. I note on a Post-it Thomas's argument that some animals who may become extinct are protected in zoos. This discussion could go on for awhile. We have been studying mammals for several weeks, and the children are beginning to internalize information and make important connections on some real issues.

Knowing that the children will get wiggly soon, Jane flips through the chart papers to reveal the morning's message. Today it is about the mammal research that we will be doing next during Investigations Workshop time.

January 25

Dear Children,

    The mammal research is g _____ well. We see that you are making interesting dis _____ about your mammals. We hope that you finish t _____ notes at Investigations today, so that y _____ can begin to fill out your Project Plan paper. The mammal presentations will be on Fr _____. We are looking forward to them!

Love,
Jane and Penny

The children know that the first thing Jane will ask for is a summary of the message. They study it, some reading it silently, while others look to pick out words that they recognize. Jane calls on two children to offer their summaries. Five-year-old Miranda tells us, "It is about mammals." Rebecca, a third-year student, elaborates, "We will be working in our mammal research groups today to get ready for our presentations on Friday." I see Lewis writing furiously on his Post-its. He knows good summaries when he hears them!

The lesson continues, and the children read the message aloud in unison. Together we decide which words make sense to put in the missing blanks. For the next ten minutes the children will examine reading, writing, and spelling strategies, as we spell the missing words and discuss the content of the message. The message format provides students with many opportunities for gaining literacy. As we spell, we discuss consistencies and vagaries of the sound/symbol correspondence of standard spelling. We compare "sound spellings" to the conventional spellings of words. We then ask children to point out interesting things they have noticed on the message. Again, children approach this task at their own levels. Today Justin, an advanced reader, points out that the word *investigation* is formed by adding the suffix *tion* to the root word *investigate*. Sasha, an emergent reader, comes to the chart and proudly circle all the *e*'s she has found. As we review the chart, we spend time focusing on phonics and mechanics. We may talk briefly about word patterns, rhymes, homophones, vowel combinations, consonant blends, or the structural features of punctuation and capitalization. We also use the message to consider other areas of written expression, such as word choice, sentence structure, and grammatical usage. The contents of each individual message, along with the students' ideas, dictate the day's lesson.

At the end of the lesson Lewis and I, the observers, spend a few minutes reading from our Post-its, pointing out the positive things we have observed as we watched. Later the Post-its will be filed in each child's individual section of the class record book. We refer to notes in these books when we confer with parents. The children have access to the books as well; they love to read about the great things they are doing.

A copy of the message goes home daily with every child for homework. Children and parents work on homework together. Since children are working at different levels, parents participate in the homework assignment in different ways. Depending on the child's facility with reading and writing, the parents' responsibilities range from reading the message out loud and writing the words in the blanks as the child supplies them, to listening and watching as the child completes the work independently. Simply by becoming involved in the homework process, parents can see how their children progress throughout the year. And, since the messages are always relevant to the goings-on of the classroom, participating in the homework lesson is a good way for parents to stay informed about school activities.

10:00 A.M.

The children are definitely ready to move by this time. They get their Investigations Logs out of their cubbies and quickly sort themselves into their mammal research groups. This time we have designed these groups of three to be multiaged with at least one advanced reader in each group. Half of the groups stay in Jane's room, and the other half come to mine. Each group finds its pile of research materials where it is stored on a shelf and settles down to work. The research is taking different forms. Some children listen as another child reads aloud. Some children take notes, drawing and writing in their Investigations Logs. Other children discuss their mammal and plan what they will do for their exhibition on Friday. One group argues about who will do what during this research session.

I move around the room trying to be helpful. I show a group how to use the index in a book. I explain to another group how to take notes in an abbreviated form to save time. I make a general announcement reminding the children to get a snack from the basket. I help another group read a difficult passage. I go to the arguing group to offer my assistance and find that they are drawing straws to decide who will be the reader today. Now if they can only decide who will draw first, everything will be hunky dory!

In our multiage class we have always used thematic units to integrate the curriculum. We can hash over the subject matter together in a large group and then deal with it at a more individual level at Investigations and Communications Workshops. Our school district requires that we teach some of our themes. We have big manuals that go with our science curriculum with lots of suggested activities. However, we find that we rarely use these activities. Instead, we like to use the children's questions and ideas to guide us as we plan our own activities. In my journal I describe how we got going on the mammal theme a couple of weeks ago:

January 7

We are always trying to find ways to get the kids more involved in determining the curriculum. Our problem is that we think they have to have a certain bit of background knowledge before they can state their needs and interests. Each message this week has been about some aspect of what we know or what we want to know about mammals. On Monday, we introduced the new theme with a poem and worked on figuring out the characteristics of mammals. We also asked the children a question and encouraged them to talk it over with their parents: Why do you think we should study about mammals? Maybe a fourth of the children discussed this with their families and wrote ideas down on the backs of their homework papers. We shared these ideas at message time on Tuesday. We'd like to get more family participation like this. In Tuesday's message we asked the children to talk with their families about what kinds of activities we could do to find out about mammals. We told them we were going to have a class meeting on Wednesday to discuss their suggestions. More kids came in with ideas on their homework on Wednesday. We videotaped the meeting—it adds value to something to videotape it, we think. They had many good suggestions for activities.

Today we did an activity about the various ways mammals move. (Leslie had suggested that we "act out" mammals to learn about them.) We tried to bring out how mammals have adapted in differing ways to their environment. Their strategies for getting food and staying safe from predators vary. The kids acted out the movements, which is the part they liked, while we tried to sneak some learning in there. The next step is to find out the kids' questions. They have been alerted on their homework to come with some tomorrow. We'll write them in our Investigations Logs. Hopefully, we can marry the questions with their ideas for activities and come up with a fairly child-centered approach to this whole thing. We want to keep coming back to the *Why* question—Why should we study mammals? Next week we'll get involved with setting up an authentic play area in the Little Room.

I look around the room. There is a lot of evidence of the children's involvement in this theme: habitat murals on the walls, pictures describing characteristics of mammals, a decorated list of reasons why we should study mammals. On the door of the Little Room, an area that connects our two classrooms, is a painstakingly fashioned sign: *Mammal Laboratory—Opened in January.* Inside the lab are numerous kid-fashioned tools for studying mammals, both alive and dead, along with pictures, maps, and posters. The set of shelves we have designated as the multiage museum is beginning to get crowded with mammal-related things from the children's homes: books, magazine and newspaper articles, a steel trap, a model of a whale, a mink's tail. The research that the students are doing right now is an activity suggested by one of the children. I suspect that the learning going on here surpasses that detailed as objectives in our curriculum guide. In addition to learning facts about mammals, the children are learning *how* to learn. As I stop by the group that is researching whales Benny comments to me, "It's a good thing that big kids are here. Because if they weren't, we wouldn't know what to do so much." I am glad that one day Benny will have the chance to be one of the big kids in this class. Our work on designing curriculum will continue to grow as he does.

10:50 A.M.

The children gather up their research materials and pile them on the shelves. It is math time. Again, the children sort themselves into groups. More than half of them go to Jane's room. Until now, our first-year students have gone home just before the formal math time. Today, all the youngest ones are going to work with Jane, expanding the range of developmental levels that she will need to address.

Jane will work with her whole group for a time to create a *Mammals as Pets* graph. Then she will allow the children to freely investigate the baskets of manipulatives to finish out the math period. The older children in the room never tire of playing with the assorted collections of objects, blocks, and shapes. In their play they will introduce ideas and relationships to the younger students as they continue to make discoveries themselves. Jane needs some time to observe and talk with the youngest students as they explore patterns and numbers, so that she can begin to design activities based on their needs.

In my room my group gathers on the rug. I page through *The World Book Encyclopedia* to show them the section on beavers and explain that beavers have always interested me. I describe the beaver dam in our swamp, and tell them that the previous night I had looked up beavers in the encyclopedia to find out more about how they hibernate. I had been amazed by the amount of numerical information the article contained. I tell the children that I sometimes forget how important numbers are for communicating information, and I show how I used this encyclopedia article to create some problems about beavers.

Mammal Math Problems
The Beaver

1. One male beaver is 96 cm. long. His mate is 91 cm. long. What is the difference in their lengths?

2. Beavers have 4 strong front teeth for gnawing and 16 back teeth for chewing. How many teeth do they have in all?

3. A beaver's tail is usually about 12 inches long and 7 inches wide. What is the difference between the length and width of the beaver's tail?

4. Thousands of years ago the beavers of North America were about 7 feet long. Nowadays beavers grow only 4 feet long. How much bigger did beavers used to be?

5. A female beaver usually has two to four kits in a litter. This is what a kit looks like. It has soft fluffy fur and its eyes are open at birth. It is 36 cm. long from the nose to the tip of its tail. Its tail is 8 cm. long. The front feet are 4 cm. long. The back feet are 8 cm. long. It weighs 1 pound. Its fur is brown. Its feet and tail are black. Draw a life-sized picture of a beaver kit.

6. Hunters in North America trap over 500,000 beavers a year. Write the number 500,000 in words.

I give the children copies of the problems and send them off to work on them. Some choose to work independently, and others pair up. As I check on their progress, I notice and comment on the strategies they are using to solve the problems. Tomorrow we will get together and explain our thinking to each other. Today, though, I leave them alone to do as much of their own thinking as possible. They are used to my responding to their questions with questions of my own. I see today that some children are still having a little trouble with the word *difference*; I had included it purposely to check on their understanding of that concept. Measuring is posing a problem for a few children, too, but I see them getting good help from each other as they do the drawing required in #5. After some discussion of the problems tomorrow, those who have finished them will choose a mammal and use the encyclopedia to create a few problems of their own. I will then type these up as a collection of mammal problems to be distributed for more practice another day.

A few years ago when Jane and I realized the extent that math workbooks were dictating our math curriculum, we abandoned them. Our district provides us with a listing of goals and objectives to cover, as well as the tests to assess these objectives. Fortunately, as in all the other subject areas, we are allowed to create our own methods for teaching the math curriculum. Even though our reading and thinking about math was pointing us in the direction of a more hands-on, child-centered, integrated approach to numeracy, it took the cold-turkey move of not ordering workbooks to spring us from our dependency.

Now, two years later, we are beginning to feel more comfortable creating curriculum with the children based on their needs as we see them. Instead of the almost daily written work that the math workbooks demanded, we are free to use paper and pencil only when the children are ready for it. We are finding that numbers fit naturally into the learning we are doing all day long.

11:25 A.M.

In our rooms after math and before going to lunch we get ready for Communications Workshop. Today, we cut math a little short, so that we can talk with the youngest children about how we will get organized. That done, we get out our writing folders and day books from our cubbies, and we select the books we plan to read at quiet reading time. Dan passes out day books to the little ones. Since we write in these journals every day, we adopted literacy educator and writer Donald Murray's name for his daily journal. We make the day books by enclosing twenty-five to thirty sheets of plain ditto paper with oak tag covers and binding these with plastic binders. "Do you want blue, green, or yellow?" Dan conscientiously asks each child. Each of us decides where we would like to sit today, and we pile our stuff in that spot. As usual, Serene is at the table next to the window. Susan is encouraging Tara to join her on the pillows by the kneeling table. Hannah is off by herself at a small table by the museum. Dan and Tracy are together in the little office-like nook behind the science bookshelf. Heidi has saved a place for me at the table with bigger chairs. Thank you, Heidi!

There are nooks and crannies and open spaces in our rooms. The heights of the tables and chairs vary to accommodate all of our different sizes. There are no assigned seats and no teacher's desks. We find our places in the rooms according to our working and socializing needs of the moment. We find that it is easier to maintain fluid groupings when people do not feel possessive about their spaces.

We link the younger kids up with older partners to help them at lunch time, and then we make our trek to the cafetorium. It is a hike in our large school of 850 students. Jane and I leave our children at the lunchroom door, feeling secure that the little ones will do fine with the support of all of our lunch time veterans. We hurry back to my room for twenty minutes of talk as we eat, compare notes on the morning, and plan for the afternoon. We expect the little ones to crash at some point, but so far they are energetic and enthusiastic. Communications Workshop, which is coming up, is a large block of time with many procedural details for the children to absorb. We decide to simplify it today. We will start with quiet reading as usual, go into a mini-lesson to explain the day books, and end up with a sharing time. Today we will skip the after-day-books time, in which children choose from a variety of literacy activities. We'll neglect goal-setting with the older ones this afternoon, too, so that we will be able to get around to many of the children to hear their day-book stories and to respond to them. These decisions made, we go to collect the children from the lunchroom. No one seems to have suffered any ill effects!

12:05 P.M.

Quiet reading always happens right after lunch. Nowadays, we are reading for twenty to twenty-five minutes. It's a peaceful way to wind down after lunch, and everyone is doing just what they need to do to become better readers—*reading*! I get my novel out of my bag and settle down next to Heidi with a little trepidation today, wondering how long our little ones will last. They seem to take their cues from the rest of us, however. When they look around, they see everyone engrossed in their books. Chester is so immersed in a chapter book that he is oblivious to the rest of the world. Dan and Tracy are paging through nonfiction books from the mammal display and surreptitiously pointing out pictures of interest to each other. Justin's lips move as he reads through a pile of little predictable books at breakneck speed. The youngest children turn to their books, too, and we maintain reasonable quiet for fifteen minutes. In time, the little ones will learn that this quiet period is sacred for most of us.

When I ask the children to come to the rug for the mini-lesson, some of the children tear themselves reluctantly from their books. It is not that mini-lessons are repellent; they are short and sweet enough to be palatable for just about everyone. I remind the children that when the mini-lesson is over, they can go back to finish their reading if they are at a place where they cannot possibly stop. Today the children conduct the mini-lesson by explaining the day books to the younger students. Their instructions are all variations on the same theme: "In your day book you write about something important to you." Gregory adds earnestly, "The kids choose their own topics. Kids pick, because then they will know what to write about. If teachers tell them a topic, they won't know what to say about it." Other days we use simple lessons to address facets of literacy to help the children become better readers and writers. Having the lesson come between reading and writing makes it easy to concentrate on an aspect from either area. Sometimes, Jane and I get our two groups together and demonstrate a skill, technique, strategy, or procedure for the mini-lesson. We can model a peer conference, showing good questions and comments, or we can model invented spelling, stressing saying the words slowly out loud to listen for the sounds. We can model reading with a friend, demonstrating how to help your partner figure out a word by skipping over it and reading ahead. Short lessons such as these are particularly well-suited to multiage classes. Since individual students will absorb *what* they need from a lesson *when* they need it, we frequently repeat variations of lessons. That's okay; we've got the time.

After the day book explanation, some of us tell what we are planning to write about today. Typically, many of the stories that were told at Talking Journal time in the mornings reappear as drawings and writings in day books in the afternoons. The children return to their work places to write, the little ones eager to christen their new day books. The paper is unlined so that children are free to design their drawings and writings according to their needs. Beginning writers can use as much space as they need for their pictures, scribble writing, or labels. Advanced writers can rule their own papers with appropriately spaced lines. They can lay out their stories and illustrations on each page as they see fit.

We start with ten minutes of quiet writing time so that everyone can organize their thoughts and begin their work. After that quiet time, I put aside my day-book story about the antics of my new kitten, and I begin to move around the room. We are buzzing now. Krista is sound spelling *Pink Panther*, saying it over and over. She's got *pink* (Pingk), but *panther* is bothering her. Tanya tries to help, "Does it have an *e*?" Barry is keeping an eye on Darcy, making suggestions about capital letters. Tara is making some letter-like configurations to go with her picture. Eric chews on his pencil as he tries to dream up another wild adventure to put in his superhero story. Susan returns to the room. She has been working with a sixth grader from an upstairs classroom to edit one of her day-book stories to get it ready for publication. She shows me her story and says proudly, "Finished!"

"Great! Put your day book in my bag after sharing, and I will type your story tonight if I have time," I respond. I spend fifteen minutes listening to children read their work and talk about it; I write short messages to respond to their writing in their day books. Then I call them to the rug for sharing, before they get too involved in after-day-book activities. Normally when children finish their day books they move to another literacy activity, such as reading with each other, collaborating on research projects, going to the library, alphabetizing the homework papers, making posters, writing letters, or listening to books at the listening station. Today, however, we will have a long sharing time. During sharing the children and I read what we have written that day, and the listeners give feedback. Sometimes, too, students tell about books they have read, or read aloud from books they have particularly enjoyed.

Carter sits in the sharing chair first and reads from his day book. "Different colored crayons. Crayons made of wax," he reads as he looks over the top of his paper at his audience. Carter then shows us the three pages he has worked on during Communications Workshop. One page shows a row of different colored lines. A page of Ninja Turtles is next, and last is a full page of letters interspersed with dots.

"Any questions or comments?" Carter asks. He points to one of the raised hands, "You!"

"I like the way you did your pictures," Nan comments.

"What do you like about Carter's pictures?" I push.

"They're colorful," Nan adds.

"You!" Carter points again at a face behind the sea of waving hands.

"I like how you told crayons were made of wax," Roger says.

I smile and nod as Carter surrenders the sharing chair to another reader. "Yes, Carter's story about crayons has some interesting details, doesn't it?" I add.

The group share-session continues, with children reading and receiving feedback on their pieces. I raise my hand when I want to comment, as well, and sometimes I am chosen. However, I do speak out often during share time, usually to ask the responder to be more specific in his or her comments: "*Why* do you like the way Hannah wrote it?" or

"*What* words did Tracy use that were good words?" I'm pushing the children to avoid blanket statements such as "I liked the words she used" and "I liked his pictures." I want them to identify what part of a piece spoke to them as listeners. I also encourage the children to tell how the writing *affected* them. I model for them: "When Jeff described how his new toy worked, I could really picture it in my mind." By sharing in a large group, we all get to hear each other's comments. We practice giving meaningful feedback. Later on, we often see evidence that the children have picked up on some of the ideas that were voiced at sharing time and incorporated them into their writing.

1:30 P.M.

It's recess time! Yay! It will be an inside recess today, because the temperature has not managed to climb above ten degrees and the wind is howling. Inside recess is no problem for the kids, though Jane and I could use a breather. The older children know that inside recess is a wide-open Choice Time, and they quickly busy themselves. I look around to make sure that the younger children are occupied, too, and I see many multiaged groups of children from both classrooms playing together. A group of girls is playing house in one corner. Thomas and Tracy are in the mammal laboratory, conducting experiments. A group of children of all ages has started a game of Monopoly. A third-year student, Gregory, is teaching Zack, a five-year-old, the puppet show that he created last week. There is a group having a riotous time with the dress-ups; Tara comes to let me admire each new outrageous get-up. There is no question about this child having fun on her first whole day of school!

1:50 P.M.

Usually in the last period of our day we have literature study groups, class meetings, or story time. But today a biology professor from Colby College, Jay Labov, has come to speak to us about mammals. As we settle the children on the floor in Jane's room, we are a bit uneasy. Maybe on this first whole day for some and with inside recess to boot, the children will be wound up and wiggly. Jay has come prepared with a riveting presentation, however, with a bat skeleton, a mother mouse with her nursing babies in a cage, and other fascinating articles to look at and touch. The children are attending well, and Jay is challenging them with questions that we had no idea they knew the answers to. One phrase comes up again and again in their responses: "I read in a book once. . . ." It is good to hear that our students are learning on their own from books. We had thought that they did not have much knowledge about mammals yet, because we had not *taught* them much. But we see that they do know a lot, reminding us again that we are not their only resources for information. They are learning from books, from each other, from television, from their families, all the time. We just need to keep them thinking and making connections.

At Jane's signal Jay announces that he has time to answer one last question. He chooses five-year-old Tanya, who asks, "How do flying squirrels fly?" Jay launches into a long, detailed explanation about how flying squirrels don't actually fly. They have skin between their legs that supports them as they *glide* from a higher point to a lower point. When he is finished, Tanya raises her hand again and says, "Actually we knew that already. We just wanted to see if *you* knew."

"Oh, so you're just testing the expert, I guess?" Jay puts his head back and roars with laughter. We feel gratified that the children are self-confident in their knowledge.

2:30 P.M.

Jay is still chuckling as he packs up his mammal paraphernalia. We ask for volunteers to help him lug things to his car, and he leaves to a chorus of "Thank you's." It is time for the End-of-the-Day Circle and my "homeroom" kids bounce back to our classroom. "Let's make a fast circle. It's almost time to go home!" I tell them. The circle time must be short today, so that we have plenty of time to get the little ones snowsuited up and on the right buses.

"Hmm . . . let's see, what is a good question for today? I know. What have you done today that you are proud of?" I write this question on the clipboard in my lap. "I saw so many wonderful things happening today. What are you proud of?"

Mary's hand is waving eagerly. She says in one breath, "I wrote a letter to Hannah and it was a whole page long, and Jane told me I am getting better on my writing and I was really proud!"

"You must have been! How about you, Dan?"

"I picked a book today that was a little challenging for me, but I got through it. It was called *I Have To Go!*"

"Was it worth all that hard work?" I ask. Dan nods his head and grins.

I write down Dan's contribution as Lisbet begins to talk. "I read a chapter book. It looked hard, but it wasn't."

"Great," I say. Then I look around the circle and ask, "Should everyone in this class be reading chapter books?"

"No!" the children answer.

"Of course not," I remind them. "Lisbet is older and she has been reading for a long time. She is reading what is right for her. Just like Dan. He read what was right for him today, too. Okay, we have time for one more. Darcy?"

"I am proud that I helped Krista put away her books at the end of Communications. She was forgetting where some of them go."

"Darcy, thank you for being so helpful today. I noticed so many of you older folks helping out the younger ones all day long. Can you help them get organized to go home, too?" I begin to pass out the homework papers and the children head for the common area to gather up their wraps and book bags. Dismissal goes without a hitch, with older children escorting younger ones to their bus lines in the common area.

3:00 P.M.

"Not a bad day at all," Jane calls to me from her room.

"Piece of cake!" I answer her.

References

MUNSCH, ROBERT. 1993. *I Have To Go!* Toronto: Annick Press.

THE WORLD BOOK ENCYCLOPEDIA. 1990. Chicago: World Book, Inc.

Our Views

Jane Doan

"I know your first name." Michael boldly greeted me on the playground. Michael's dad owns the Mom and Pop store where I buy my newspaper every morning. Although Michael was in another teacher's classroom, he was getting to know me pretty well on the playground. We had had many discussions on proper playground behavior over the past two months, and I was becoming fond of this mischievous redhead. "My dad told me your name is Jane," he stated with a sly grin.

"Of course her name is Jane," piped up Kathryn from our class. "And my other teacher is Penny," she added.

"What!" exclaimed Michael. "You call your teachers by their first names?"

"Of course," repeated Kathryn. "They are part of our class just like us."

"Wow!" was the only reply Michael could think of. It was the first time I had ever known him to be speechless.

Learners Together

That the children call us by our first names is just one of the outward signs of our educational philosophy. It's difficult to be with children for a period of three or four years in a multiage setting and still be referred to as *Mrs.* The extended family relationship that a multiage classroom becomes precludes the use of titles. The closeness that comes from having the same children in our classrooms for a number of years effectively breaks down the we/they barrier that is so often present in single-grade classrooms. The friendships that evolve require the use of first names.

In the second year of our multiage program we realized that a unique relationship was developing between our students and ourselves. There was the sense of familiarity that exists when people share the same experiences on an ongoing basis. There was a closeness that comes when people work together in a caring environment. We had become more than teachers and students. We were a family. We wanted to demonstrate to the children in an outward manner that we really felt this special closeness. Since we call each other by our first names and we call the children by their first names, it seemed to follow logically that the children should call *us* by our first names.

Another reason for taking away the titles that separated us from the children was to reinforce the idea that we were all colleagues in the learning process. In our multiage classrooms everyone is not only a learner, but also a teacher. A first-name basis assures an equality that encourages everyone to take risks. We are united in working toward the same goal, the attainment of knowledge. This equality also infers that each of us is responsible for our own learning. Each of us must and can set our own educational goals. There are no "Masters" who are imparting knowledge. Each of us must work toward our own goals in learning; each of us must work to help others attain their goals. The children easily fell into the habit of calling us by our first names once we openly began referring to each other in that familiar way during the school day and signing our morning messages and parent letters with our first names.

As we have learned together with the children, our experiences have convinced us that the best teaching tool is being a learner. By modeling what we do as learners, we lead the children to become learners themselves, assuming learning strategies almost by osmosis.

Our learning over the past four years has become our philosophy. Belonging to a community of learners in a multiage environment is the mainstay of our beliefs. Other components of our philosophy of education include co-teaching, authentic learning, integrated thematic studies, student choice, a workshop format, parent involvement, and a peaceful, caring environment. We share our current views in this chapter, confident that as we continue to grow as learners we will be refining and redefining these beliefs.

Community of Learners

"How is your class really different from mine?" asks Mrs. Kinsey as we patrol the playground together during the ten minutes our recess times overlap. "I have a multiage class, too," she declares. "My first-grade students range in age from six to eight years old and there is a wide variety of ability levels in my room, too. I don't see any difference between what you do and what I am doing. All classes are multiaged!"

I nodded. "Yes. . . but, I believe the difference is that in a multiage classroom it is easier to put the emphasis on the children's needs rather than the curricular needs. When I taught in a straight second grade, I believed that I met the children's individual needs. Once I began to teach in the multiage classroom and had the opportunity to stop focusing on teaching a single grade, I realized that I had not been as individualized as I thought. I had been teaching second-grade curriculum. In a multiage class, just by the nature of the program, I am forced to focus on each child's needs rather than on the curriculum. And, of course, we have three or four years to work on these individual needs. That's a big difference right there."

Teachers often question how we think our program is different from their single-grade classrooms. Our response is always a variation of the previous one. We believe that the curriculum must be child-centered. We work in a multiage setting to make sure that we look at the children before we look at the prescribed curriculum. It is impossible for any one year's curriculum to become the driving force behind our teaching when we are faced with a class of children who range in age from five to eight. Instead, it is imperative that we look at every child as an individual and see what his or her educational requirements are.

Believing that all children learn at their own rates and have dissimilar strengths intensifies our desire to work with children in a multiage setting. We believe the best way to offer children the opportunity for supported growth at an individual pace is in a classroom where children are at different levels and where all the differences are valued. A multiage classroom does just that. In a multiage classroom each child works at his or her own pace without the fear of competition or retention. The children know they are making significant progress and that their individual progress is accepted as the norm for them. They can learn at their own rate without being considered different. They are each learners, like all the others, and their unique learning styles are treasured by their teachers and their peers. They will move on as they are ready, quickly or slowly, not in the lock-step manner of the traditional grades. Jacob, one of our second-year students, recently demonstrated his awareness of his own literacy development. During Morning Message he volunteered to spell *will*, one of the words missing on the chart. He spelled the word quickly and correctly, and Penny asked him our standard question, "How did you know how to spell that word so fast?" He replied seriously, "Well, of course I know how to spell *will*. I *was* in this class all last year and I've seen that word a lot!" Statements like this reaffirm for children that there will be time for them to learn.

The three or four years that children are with us affords us the opportunity to really know them as individuals. We are aware of their individual strengths and weaknesses. We know what works for them and what doesn't. And they know our expectations. They are successful learners because they feel safe in our program. They feel confident in their knowledge that their teachers and peers are supportive friends. As they move from being first-year students to third-year students, they see their roles in the group expand and change. They are very aware of their growth as they move along the continuum of time in the program. In addition, there are no transitions each year when they must find their place in a different room with a new teacher and new classmates. They are safe, secure, and happy with their multiage family.

With the confidence that arises from knowing one's environment, children easily assume the role of learner in our community. Their years in our multiage classroom bring them the contentment and the vigor necessary to take the risk of being learners. Their confidence within our particular program is strengthened by the fact that two teachers are available to them at all times. This co-teaching aspect of our program promotes the feeling of being learners together.

Co-teaching

One of the goals Penny and I have been working on has been to effectively co-teach. Collaborating on our multiage paper had convinced us that co-teaching was the only way to go. We had enjoyed the easy flow of ideas that being together generated. It was our belief that such "inspired" thinking would continue if we worked together in the multiage program. On the pragmatic side, we were anxious to have each other for support in our new venture.

We have found that there are many benefits of co-teaching in a multiage program. The most important is that by sharing our students we both get to know them very well. When one of us has questions or concerns about a student, the other's knowledge of that child is very helpful. For instance, when I was concerned that Fred would *never* learn to read, Penny pointed out to me all the literacy understandings Fred *was* demonstrating. I had been focusing on the negative. When I listened to Penny and focused on the positive, I found that Fred really took off. He began to see himself as a reader and writer. Without my co-teacher's knowledge of this student and her ability to gently show me what she knew, I would probably still be worrying! And I wonder how Fred would have found the support he needed to become a reader.

In order to achieve this benefit of co-teaching, it is essential for us to spend many hours together outside of the school day. One way we found to spend extra time together was to co-teach a course at the University of Maine in Orono, sixty miles from our school. This commitment required us to spend two and a half hours a week together in a car as we traveled to and from our class. These weekly trips definitely provided us with the time necessary to have relaxed conversations about the children in our program. We find that we must take time to be together. Whenever and wherever we are together our talk revolves around the practical and philosophical issues facing us in our work.

Another important aspect of co-teaching in a multiage program is that we work together planning the classroom environment that will best meet the needs of our students. The fact that there are two of us to look at our program and to think about how to make it better stimulates the kind of thinking that actually does make it better. Having two of us to question how our program benefits the children ensures that the program continues to improve. Through such inquiry we are able to continuously build on our strengths.

We began teaching the multiage program in rooms that were across the hall from each other. We gave the children the choice of being in one classroom or the other at some times during the day, but we always taught in our separate rooms. At first we both wrote our own morning messages. Later, we both did the same message, but in different rooms. Gradually, we began to combine our classes for Morning Message with one of us conducting the lesson and the other observing and writing down those observations. The observer then shared with the class the positive behaviors that she had witnessed. We found that in this way we could be very clear about our expectations for the children. We saw how eagerly the children listened to hear their names and the positive behaviors they were demonstrating. We saw our Morning Message time become an active learning time for all the children as they internalized our expectations and proudly displayed those behaviors. Morning Message time became our first true co-teaching experience.

Communications Workshop also gives us the opportunity to co-teach. Mini-lessons in reading and writing often consist of us modeling how to have a writing conference, how to share a book with a friend, or how to collaborate on a story. With two of us to role play any possible situation, the opportunities for mini-lessons are endless.

Investigations Workshops are another area in which co-teaching is an asset. We can each be working on a different project with groups of equal size. Or, one of us can conduct a scientific experiment with a small group while the other does a large group project. However the children are grouped, we try to provide opportunities for them to share their experiences with the entire multiage class.

Co-teaching offers us the opportunity to share the workload, building on each other's strengths. Penny writes the daily messages, and I write the weekly informational letters to the parents. While I am great at coming up with large global ideas for theme studies, Penny is much more adept at recognizing the teachable moments and utilizing them to the children's advantage. Penny enjoys singing and teaches many songs to the class. I much prefer to be the movement teacher, researching how to integrate exercise with each theme. Penny is an excellent storyteller and reader, so she is often in charge of our storytimes, while I listen, enjoy, and learn from her. I love to engage the children in games and add game playing to our program as often as possible. Penny is a skilled discussion leader; that task is frequently her responsibility. I am somewhat of an efficiency expert, therefore I am delegated to directing traffic! When questioned about how we co-teach, I tell people, "Penny teaches and I get things done." Seriously though, we do feel that our co-teaching allows us to utilize our individual strengths. And, perhaps more important, it gives us the opportunity to closely observe another teacher and to use these observations to become more skilled in our weaker areas. The best part of sharing the teaching load is that we both feel we are getting the best possible deal. And we know that the children are getting an even better deal than we are!

The children truly benefit from having two teachers. They know which teacher to go to in every situation. If they want an extra hug or a lap to sit on, they quickly find Penny. If it is extra recess time or more snacks that they want, they know to look for me. They all know that Penny loves to write, so questions about grammar or word usage are usually delegated to her. Since my greatest joy is to sit in a comfortable corner and read, I am often asked to help find an interesting book. Whatever the children need, they are confident that one of us will be able to meet that need for them.

Co-teaching also gives us the opportunity to constantly model for the children how two people collaborate. They watch us as we problem solve, figuring out what needs to be done next or how to handle a particular situation. They are aware of our differences, our likes and dislikes, our strengths and weaknesses. The children see how we work together to utilize each other's best attributes and how we are constantly learning from each other. These observations are internalized by the children as they work cooperatively in the multiage classroom.

Planning times and decision making come easy when there are two heads to share the thinking. Co-teaching gives our program a uniqueness that is built on our personal strengths. Together we are more than two teachers. We form a working coalition.

This working alliance expands to include the children during the school day. As members of our learning community, they give input into the long- and short-term goals of our program. The use of integrated theme studies offers our class frequent opportunities to have their say in classroom decisions.

Integrated Theme Studies

"Why should we study birds?" asks Penny at the beginning of our bird theme.

"Because if we didn't have birds then people wouldn't have invented airplanes," declares Lewis.

"Because we should know about bird beaks, and feet and what they eat and how they fly," adds Miranda.

"It's good to learn about birds because they are important to learn about," states Carter simplistically.

"I want to learn about their habitat," says Gregory.

"We should know how the birds hear the worms underground," mentions Charlie.

"We should know all about birds so that if they become endangered we will know how to help them," adds our environmentally conscious Leslie.

The children have their answers ready because this question had been posed on their homework the previous day. They are eager to discuss not only why we should study birds, but also what we should investigate about them. The children are ready to take ownership of our theme study. They pool their resources for ideas of what we need to learn and how we can go about learning it.

The broadness of our theme study allows all the children to participate. Everyone, regardless of age or ability, has a say in what will be studied. All children are able to take some knowledge of the subject and call it their own. The more knowledgeable of the children will share their expertise with those less familiar with the topic. In our multiage class the range of differences in interests as well as abilities offers all the children a more varied learning environment as we learn from each other.

The most important impetus to working together as learners is experiencing legitimate learning situations. The use of integrated theme studies facilitates authentic learning.

Real Learning for Real Reasons

The multiage group of six children look at the math question that they had posed, "How many bones are there in our classroom?"

"This is going to be hard," murmurs six-year-old Nathan.

"No," states five-year-old Fred. "We all want to know, so we will all work together and the answer will come *just like that*!"

And that is what happens. Several days later, after researching how many bones there are in one body and using place value blocks to determine how many bones there are in all our bodies combined, the group is ready to present their work and their answer to the whole class. Their display covers an entire table. Don explains proudly, "These big blocks stand for thousands. These flat ones are the hundreds. The stick is a ten and here are the ones."

Rebecca can't stand it. She interrupts, "See, there are 7,416 bones in this room!"

"Didn't we have a great question?" Leslie beams.

The children are as satisfied with their question as they are proud of their solution, for it is what they wanted to know about our class. It is important to them.

As often as possible we use learning for real reasons as the driving educational force in our class. The multiage nature of the class requires us to set aside the grade-level curriculums and to offer the children learning that is directly meaningful to them. Allowing the children to pose their own problem-solving questions, offering them the opportunity to decide the direction of our theme studies, and giving them control over what they will read and write contribute to making the school learning situation as real as possible for each child. It is our belief that children learn best when the learning is important to them, when it is real for them.

At the end of the school year we asked the children to write letters and cards to thank the many volunteers who had worked in our class. We feared that this teacher-designated task would result in careless work. Who likes to write "Thank You" notes, after all? But we were surprised. The children quickly turned the task into a meaningful experience. They saw that thanking those who worked with them was a very real task. The children learned from each other what qualities made a card interesting. After Jeff used a secret code to express his message, several others began to write in code. The first day's thank you cards contained a variation on the "Roses are red. . ." theme, and the following days' efforts turned up many more. The children wanted their cards to please their adult friends. And they did. When the volunteers read each child's card aloud and thanked the individual who wrote it, the children saw the pleasure their work gave to another person.

Recently, we met with members of the Western Maine Partnership, a consortium sponsored by the University of Maine at Farmington. At that meeting, one of the teachers, Mary Bilodeau-Callan, explained how her middle school involved the children in curriculum planning. She told us that they ask the children two questions: "What do you want to know about yourself?" and "What do you want to know about the world?" The children's responses are then used to determine the following year's curriculum. "Wow!" we thought, "Our kids could do that, too!" Up until that time we had chosen all of the themes in order to insure that we covered the required curriculum. Now, realizing that there is no set age when people suddenly are able to be responsible for their own learning, we decided it was time to give the children more control over our theme studies.

We told our students about the questions and explained that their answers would be used to determine our themes for the next school year. The children worked in groups of three or four, with the older children who would be leaving the class in June acting as facilitators for each group. Not knowing what to expect, we nervously paced the floor as the children settled into their groups and started to work. After we discussed the role of facilitators, ours took their work very seriously. They made certain that each person in the group had an opportunity to speak. They valued every answer, recording it so they would be able to report it later to the whole class. The younger children gave considerable thought to these questions and offered what they truly wanted to know. Later, the entire group of children sat quietly in a large circle listening as each small group shared its findings. The children were pleased and proud that they were allowed a say in determining the next year's curriculum. They saw this task as real. And we believe that next year, when they are studying the themes of their choice, they will be thoroughly involved in themes that now have real meaning for them.

Student Choice

The students surround the two large pieces of paper, one of which is labeled, "Communications Workshop—Penny's Room," the other, "Communications Workshop—Jane's Room." Some sign their names quickly, knowing exactly the room of their choice. Others are more thoughtful, weighing all the variables, deciding just what would be best for them for the next two weeks. Regardless of personal style or the reasons for their selection, all the children are making a choice as to where they wish to do their writing and reading.

We offer the children as many choices as possible. The children choose rooms to work in, where they want to sit, which activities to do, what research to pursue, which topics to write about, which math problems to solve, and which books to read. This emphasis on personal choice reflects our belief that children must be allowed to have ownership over their own learning. Allowing choice becomes easy in our multiage classroom because the children already know that everyone is different and that different choices are valued.

Choice Time presents the children with an easy introduction to the idea that they can decide for themselves which learning activity they would like to pursue. Each Choice Time offers the children a selection of possibilities. Their decisions are made more difficult by the fact that they can choose with whom they wish to work, and often they may choose where they want to work. The older children assist the younger children, reading the day's offerings and giving their suggestions for what might be interesting for each child. Younger children rapidly take charge of their own decisions and begin to offer suggestions to their older peers.

Literature groups become an important arena in which the children make choices. We present five books to the class, and the children select the book they would prefer to read and discuss on literature group days for a three-week period. There is much discussion as the children help one another to make the most appropriate choice.

"Oh, I read *Blueberries for Sal* before," exclaims seven-year-old Laura. "You'll love it, Dan. It has bears in it."

"*Miss Rumphius* is wonderful," gushes Rebecca, one of our third-year students. "I think it is the best book ever. I just know that you will like it, Nan."

"Why don't we sign up together for *One Morning In Maine*," Jeff suggests to Justin. "It is by Robert McCloskey. He wrote *Make Way for Ducklings* too, and you liked that book."

Whenever there is a choice to be made, the advantages of being in a multiage classroom are apparent. There are always children who are more experienced and are able and willing to advise their peers. They accept their role as counselors and are generous with their assistance.

A Caring, Family Environment

Miranda's legs dangle from the author's chair. She looks especially tiny sitting there today, ready to share her first story with words to the class. "I have a flower," she reads. And she shows the class her picture and her writing, "I hv a flr." Thomas jumps up and gives her a hug. "I really like that you wrote the words!" he gleefully exclaims. Then he quickly adds, "I like the way you took your time on your picture too!" Miranda beams. Thomas is her special friend, but he also is one of the advanced writers in the class. It is with his encouragement that she has been able to take the risk to sound spell the story she wished to write. His support of her as a storyteller when she drew and explained her pictures encouraged her to take the leap to writing words.

The children know that they can count on each other for support in their efforts to become better scholars. The knowledge that the other children in the class are backing them up relieves much of the stress that comes with taking risks. The knowledge that the other students care that they make an effort in their struggle to learn promotes risk taking.

Roger confidently raises his hand at message time. He knows that he can spell that word. He wants to be called on. He wants to give it a try. His eagerness captures Penny's attention. "Roger, come up here and spell this word for us," she invites. Roger boldly walks to the chart at the front of the class. "B," he begins.

"Listen, *band*," Penny encourages. "What sounds do you hear?"

"B d" Roger replies, a little less confidently.

"Say it out loud," urges Penny. "Say it slowly and listen to the sounds."

"Band, b n d," tries Roger. "Almost!" cheers Penny. "You need a vowel. Try again."

Roger looks thoughtful. Then his eyes light up. "B A N D," he spells. And the class spontaneously claps in appeciation of his successful struggle. Proudly, Roger returns to his place.

In a multiage class, because there is a wide range of differences in ages and abilities, there is also a wide acceptance of these differences. The children support each other as risk takers and celebrate each other's successes. Every child feels valued. This acceptance of individual differences happens, we believe, because of the class's diversity. In a multiage setting the children see clearly that everyone does not need to be alike. They understand that each person's uniqueness contributes positively to the class. Because there is no grade norm as there is in a traditional class, the children quickly come to know that they can be who they are. And they just as quickly realize that the other children can be who they are, too. This knowledge results in a caring, supportive environment. It's more like a family than a class.

Such an affectionate, appreciative setting is perfect for a class based on a workshop format. Children who are accustomed to working cooperatively together are able to appreciate and utilize the freedom a workshop gives them. Immersion in a family environment such as this results in support for everyone's endeavors.

Workshop Format

"Jacob, can you help me, please," asks Benny. "I can't find any paper to make a poster."

"Of course," replies Jacob. "What is your poster going to be about?"

"I want to make a poster of mammals who live in the water. You know, whales and dolphins."

"Don't forget otters, and beavers, too," counsels Jacob. "Hey, could I work on the poster with you?"

"Sure, you can help. Let's work at the table in the Little Room. Then we will have privacy."

It's Communications Workshop time and Jacob and Benny have finished writing in their day books. They are free to work on one of several after-day-book activities. They can choose to write a letter, or to read a book either quietly by themselves or with a friend. They can listen to books on tape or they can tape themselves reading a book. They can write a story, either alone or collaboratively. They can develop a play or a puppet show for presentation to the class. This time is theirs to work with as they please. The only requirement is that they work on some aspect of communications.

If you visit our classroom it might seem that our decision to use a workshop format rather than to use a learning-center approach based on specific tasks happened because of the lack of space in which to put centers. Our philosophical basis for this conclusion stems from our appreciation of children's individual differences. The wide range of differences in attitudes, abilities, and interests in a multiage classsroom calls for an educational setting that is able to meet the greatest variety of student needs. In a learning-center approach the tasks are often teacher-directed; the student has little choice in how to proceed. A workshop format provides a wide array of possible approaches to a task, allowing for opportunities for student choice. In truth, these choices are often limited only by the individual's imagination and the academic area around which the workshop is based.

A workshop format is welcoming to parents, too. It offers parents the opportunity to share with the children their ideas for activities on a particular theme. The informal atmosphere of the workshop encourages parent participation.

Parent Involvement

"Lend me your ears, me mates, and I'll tell the story of how I found this treasure map," growled the wild-haired, scar-faced pirate. The children, seated on the darkened stage where they had discovered this amazing individual, were all eyes as well as all ears. As he began his story there was not an inattentive child present. When he finished and offered to lead them through the last few steps to the treasure, every child was ready to follow.

This treasure hunt, the culminating activity to our map study, was arranged completely by parents. They made the maps, found eye patches for each child, and helped the children to read the map keys and follow the maps to find the location of the treasure. Several days' work was put into this effort by the parents, and the children learned that they could read and follow maps. And they had fun.

Involving parents in our program is one of the major commitments we made when we began our multiage program. We insisted from the start that it be a parent-choice program. We believe that when parents look at the educational programs being offered and choose one that meets their child's and their own needs, they immediately become empowered. They know from the day they register their child for school that they are partners in the education of that child. They know that they are expected to participate as fully as possible in the schooling of their child. They know that they must take responsibility for seeing that the program they chose provides the best possible educational environment for their child.

Before each school year begins, we have a meeting with the parents of all the children in the program. At this meeting the parents are asked to write down three goals for their child for this particular school year. We use these goals as an aid in meeting the individual needs of our students.

At this meeting we also ask for parent volunteers in our class. We are specific about the kind of help we need and the times we need help. Training sessions are offered so that parents will feel confident when they arrive in the classroom to work with literature groups or to help during Communications or Investigations Workshops. Parents who previously volunteered in these positions help us conduct these mini-seminars, giving firsthand accounts of the importance of the volunteers in the classroom.

Scheduled conferences with our parents begin in mid-October and are repeated in the spring. We schedule two or three conferences a week at times convenient for the parents. An hour-long block of time is allotted for each conference to allow the parents time to feel comfortable enough to ask the hard questions. We have found that after about twenty minutes parents find the confidence to question the why's of our program and how specific school experiences benefit their child. They are able to tell us what they see working for their child, as well as what they see not working. Together we are able to assess whether their child is moving toward achieving the goals set by parents and teachers alike. Together we are able to modify the program, making adjustments that will best benefit their child.

Periodically throughout the year, we send home a parent survey asking parents what they are happy about, what they are concerned about, and what they want to know more about (see Appendix B). We use these surveys to discover areas of parental concern and to gain information that will help us modify the program.

Weekly parent newsletters share information about our current theme work, our field trips, and our guest speakers (see Appendix C). Through this newsletter we ask for parent input and help in our theme studies. We have been fortunate to have parents with a wide range of interests and areas of expertise. One has been willing to lead a discussion on birds, and another has shared his knowledge of rocks and minerals. Others have come into school to tell about their occupations or have invited us to their workplaces. We have learned about forestry, horticulture, electricity, and seed trials. We have visited the family practice office of a doctor parent and enjoyed hands-on experiences with many of the tools of his trade. The children have explored these and many other topics with the help of the parents.

Our goal in teaching a multiage classroom is to provide a natural environment in which children can acquire knowledge. We are trying to create classrooms that look and act much less like a traditional school. We are trying to remember that we are dealing with human beings. Life outside the classroom is multiaged. People learn together and collaborate in their work. Work is done for very real reasons. People care for one another and nurture each other. We are trying to make our classrooms function as much like the real world as possible.

This chapter has presented our current views of appropriate educational practices in a multiage setting. We have seen and read about many other very successful programs, and we have taken all that we have learned and blended it together to formulate a philosophy that fits our needs and those of the children we teach. We expect that as we meet with other multiage educators and read about other programs, our views will keep changing to accomodate our new knowledge.

References

COONEY, BARBARA. 1982. *Miss Rumphius*. New York: Viking Press.

McCLOSKEY, ROBERT. 1941. *Make Way for Ducklings*. New York.: Viking Press.

——— . 1948. *Blueberries for Sal*. New York: Viking Press.

——— . 1952. *One Morning in Maine*. New York: Viking Press.

Valuing

Penelle Chase

When we planned this book, we thought long and hard about topics to include. We thumbed through many teacher books, looking at chapter titles and debating. It seemed that "Classroom Management" and "Student Assessment" were hot topics; all the books had chapters devoted to these areas. During one of our sessions I grumbled to Jane, "Both of these areas are about control. They are about controlling kids' behavior and their learning. Might as well call chapters like these 'How to Make the Kids Do What They're Supposed to Do' and 'How to Test Them After They've Done It.' Forget it!"

Jane laughed briefly, and then she grew serious. "I don't see any way around it, Penny. We can't write a book about education without talking about behavior and evaluation. It's not that these areas aren't important to us. It's just that we approach them differently. As multiage teachers we have more options."

"What do you mean?"

"Think about it. We have our students for three or sometimes four years. As they mature we work *with* them toward the goal of responsible behavior. And as for evaluation, we teach them to evaluate their own learning."

"You're right, Jane. And in a multiage context we have the elements of continuity, group stability, and time on our side!"

"Yes!" Jane said. "I knew you could get fired up about these topics! Say, how about you writing this part. I'll help you with the chapter titles."

"Thanks, Jane."

Jane *was* right. We would have to deal with these issues in our book. People would be eager to know how it is possible to keep track of the disparate social and academic developmental levels of children in a multiage class. So, what could we call our chapters? We batted possibilities around, dismissing one after another as quickly as we voiced them. Management. Discipline. Classroom Control. Organization. Assessment.

Testing. None of these terms rang true. Instead, they suggested that control of behavior and learning was in the hands of the teachers, rather than the students. Having recently been students ourselves at the University of Maine, the memory of how that felt was fresh in our own minds. In my journal I remembered how we had grappled with assessment issues that directly affected us, and how our instructor, Brenda Power, had helped us resolve them.

Brenda Power leaned forward in her chair and looked intently at the eight women sitting around the table. "Since this portfolio will be an evaluation instrument for literacy graduate students, perhaps we can start by sharing what we value in the literacy program here. If we start with what we value as learners, I think the list we generate will help us to design a portfolio to support these principles."

Jane and I had come eagerly to this first meeting of the portfolio development group, and we saw right away that we were not going to be disappointed. Dr. Brenda Power could very well be our savior! We were nearing the end of our Master's program, and the dreaded Comprehensive Exam was looming. "Better start forming your study groups soon," our professors had advised us. This test was a killer. You were in a room all by yourself for four hours, with just pencil and paper. No books, no resources. Well, maybe a dictionary. But that was *all*! You had to know who was important in literacy education and why, and you had to be able to write fast to build a coherent argument to address the issues put forth in the exam questions. Heaven help you if you couldn't work under pressure!

The Comprehensive Exam did not jibe with anything we had been taught about assessing literacy. Throughout our coursework we had been given a large degree of personal ownership of our work, in deciding on both the processes and the products that would best fit our needs as learners. Our professors had lived and learned about teaching literacy *with* us throughout the course of our study. None of them had felt the need for formal assessment in any of our classes. Our talk, our journal writing, and our creations were authentic demonstrations of our learning. What right or motive did they have for imposing a test upon us now? It didn't make sense. Besides being terrified, we were rebelling philosophically.

Like an answer to our prayers, here was Brenda, new kid at the University of Maine and ready to take on the system and create another option for the Master's in Literacy exit requirement. But she was not going to do it alone. Everyone at the table that night heard Brenda's use of the pronoun *we. We* were being given the opportunity to assume the final responsibility for our work. Brenda, our teacher, would help us.

The value statements flew around the table. "We value the opportunity to be in charge of our own learning, at our own pace." "We value learning as a lifelong process." "We value the opportunity to make choices." "We value the freedom that comes from being a learner, rather than only a teacher." "We value process in education." "We value the opportunity to talk with other people and share ideas." "We value the resources and learning that happens outside of school." I watched Jane breathe a long sigh and sit back in her chair. "Ah, this is more like it," I thought to myself. "This is what evaluation is all about."

Discussing chapter titles, Jane and I now realized that Brenda's brainstorming exercise had become the essence of our educational philosophy. It is our values that govern both our social and academic learnings. We suddenly saw that "values" would be the masthead of a single chapter that focused on student responsibility for behavior and on self-evaluation. We mapped out the chapter, "Valuing," to include several aspects of values in our program. First, we would show how we work at becoming a community with common values. Then, we would look at the children's learning and discuss the evaluation process, both from the students' viewpoints and from our vantage points as teachers. We heaved a sigh of relief. Maybe those two tricky issues, management and assessment, which are the crux, it seemed, of what every teacher wants to know, wouldn't be so messy to deal with after all.

The Community's Values

Karen Simpson, a multiage teacher from Hallowell, Maine, spent a day in our classroom recently. Immersed in her first year of multiage teaching, she had come to gather tips on management, scheduling, curriculum, whatever. The talk between the three of us after school was rich and good. She was impressed with the tone of our class. "How do you get the children to be so caring, so positive with each other?" she wondered. Jane and I looked at each other and thought, "Hmm, lucky she came on one of the good days!" However, Karen's question forced us to think. How *does* our group move toward becoming a community with shared values?

For example, one day Jeff and Barry collided and fell in a heap as they were heading for their cubbies. Jeff said first, "Are you all right?" and Barry answered, "Yes, are you?" Neither of them was hurt; they were laughing. Still, it was good to hear them voicing concern for each other. Jeff and Barry are both third-year students in our program. They have participated in the class rule-setting sessions each fall. They have seen the list of agreed upon rules dwindle dramatically over the years. In their first year Jeff and Barry provided input as the class created a long, complicated list of guidelines with accompanying positive and negative consequences. Because that long list proved to be so cumbersome, in their second year they eagerly helped to pare the list down to what we all thought were the *essential* five or six rules for classroom behavior. But even this simple list had its drawbacks. Some rules didn't apply in all situations. "Raise your hand to speak" actually meant raise your hand to speak only when we were in a large group situation, not when we were talking to each other during a workshop. Some rules were open to interpretation. "Be a good friend" sounded good, but what did it mean? Some rules were missing. "Throw away your used tissues; don't leave them on the rug for someone else to deal with." How could we have forgotten to put that one on our list? So, even though we had the list, no one ever referred to it or thought much about it. We were functioning fairly well as a community, because we all really knew how to act if we stopped to think about it. The only trouble was that it seemed to be the adults who were spending a lot of time reminding kids to think about their behavior. If anyone behaved inappropriately, he or she was invited by an adult to choose a better way of acting. If that resolve failed, the student spent some time in a designated planning chair figuring out a plan of behavior so he or she could rejoin the group. The planning chair system was definitely the teacher input piece of the rule chart, and that seemed to be the only element of the list that was in operation.

As we began the year the next fall we looked at the old list with dissatisfaction. We wanted the creation of standards for behavior to be a joint effort; we wanted everyone in the group to have a voice in this all-important issue. We wanted everyone, not just the adults, to feel responsible for conduct. What could we do to make our guidelines more meaningful?

During that goal-setting meeting we showed the previous year's list to the children and expressed our concerns. What rules do we *need* so that we can all get along happily here? After talking for a little while and thinking back over the past, together we came up with the all-encompassing philosophy that we live by nowadays: "Treat others the way you would like to be treated." We realize that this philosophy is not a new outlook on life; children are taught it in homes, churches, and classrooms around the world. The universality of the concept makes it a natural end result of a discussion of rules. But the beauty of it as a modus operandi in a classroom is that it applies to every possible situation. You listen to others because you would like others to listen to you. You don't get in front of someone else in line, because you would hate it if someone cut you. You help someone with a math problem, because you yourself might need some help someday. You talk in a quiet voice during a working time, because you would not appreciate someone speaking loudly around you when you were trying to concentrate. You take care of your own used tissues, because you would be disgusted to find someone else's dirty tissues in your environment. This philosophy covers everything!

By now the children in our classroom have heard the "treat others" statement many times. The older children have had the responsibility of introducing the philosophy to the younger children; they have modeled it and explained how it works. We can all recite it and understand what it means. That, at least, is a step in the right direction. Because the rule is simple to say and easy to remember we can devote our energies to following it. And because our children are with us year after year they have less chance of forgetting it. We hope that over time, caring is becoming more and more naturally ingrained in all of our value systems.

We are all human, however, and we are not perfect. I lectured Eric and Gregory at math time the other day. They were giggling at Leslie who was struggling with a math concept. "In here we don't laugh at people who are using their brains to think. We don't make fun if people make mistakes. Because that's not the way you would like to be treated. And here we treat others the way we would like to be treated." My message was clear, and I didn't mess around delivering it. The boys were chagrined. I spoke out strongly because I felt strongly. But it just happened that I was the one to speak out that day. Another time one of the kids might have been the first to say, "Hey, that's not very nice! Is that the way you would like to be treated?" Another time Eric or Gregory might have been the ones to remind any one of us to consider another person's feelings. Though we all occasionally do some unkind things, unkindness is not pervasive in our rooms. We believe that taking time to state expectations for caring pays off. Maybe way back in their subconscious minds Jeff and Barry were thinking about the class philosophy when they treated each other with care after their collision. We see that concern for others is slowly increasing year by year, as we have the stability of a core of children in the multiage classroom who keep hearing this message from us and from each other.

Caring about ourselves and about others is all we are really aiming for in our multiage classroom. It is not our wish to create a classroom management plan, a discipline plan, or a set of strategies for manipulating kids. If we enter into the classroom with the idea that we will control children or *make* them behave we are not allowing them to make decisions for themselves. We want no part of the we/they dichotomy that is traditional, but lamentable, in schools. That dichotomy goes like this: We make the rules; they obey them. We decide on the curriculum; they learn it. We give the assignment; they have it in on time. We talk; they listen. We praise; they preen. We compare; they compete. Schools do not have to operate in such a one-sided fashion. With permission and practice children can help to set standards of behavior, to determine curriculum, to regulate their own learning, and to establish community values. The teacher does not always have to be the one in charge. Sometimes kids teach the lessons.

During a recent mini-lesson children were sharing aloud the goals they would concentrate on for the next two weeks in Communications Workshop. Barry had an editing goal. He read it off: "I will work on editing one of my stories for publication." Then he added, "But I don't really know much about how to edit and publish." I assured him that someone would help him with that part once he had chosen a story that he valued.

Then Tracy announced conversationally, "I don't know what this editing and publishing stuff means either." He was promptly squelched by Gregory who lit into him, berating him for not listening to Penny and Jane, who had talked about editing and publishing many times, and for not noticing all the people who were publishing books around him. Seeing the look on Tracy's face, I opened my mouth ready to launch into a little speech about how Tracy would understand this process when he was ready to use it. But Dan beat me to it, defending Tracy vigorously. I sat back to listen. Dan was saying, "Probably he just forgot what it was. He is younger than you, Gregory. I bet you didn't know what editing and publishing were last year! And so what if you did! Probably Tracy will be editing one of his Batman stories pretty soon." Other children nodded their heads in agreement.

"That takes care of that," I thought. Another child began to talk about her goals while I marveled at the interaction I had just witnessed. Not only had Dan responded spontaneously to the injustice of Gregory's remarks, he had voiced one of the major tenets of the multiage philosophy: learners learn differently. Dan, not the teacher, assumed the responsibility of making sure that everyone understood. Dan knew that his voice was as important as any other voice in the room.

Children find security in a multiage environment. The new children join the group in the fall knowing that they are in for a long-term commitment. The sense of history is evident. The new children recognize that there is a large contingent of their classmates that already knows the ropes, that remembers events that happened last year or the year before, and that has fairly accurate expectations for the way things will go this year. There are no nervous older children on the first day of school! Their natural easiness and confidence rubs off on the new younger children. However, the older students know that they have some responsibilities toward our new class members, as well. Particularly at the beginning of the year, we count on them to help the little ones feel comfortable at school. They rise to their responsibilities admirably. Purposefulness is a good feeling, and it is easy to come by in a multiage grouping where there are younger children needing reassurance.

It takes time and stability for caring to happen. That is one reason why a multiage class lends itself to gaining values. Like any family does, we work on values constantly. We have the luxury of time. Because we are always learning a bit more about how to get along with each other, we know that the time we spend on values will be a good investment for the years to come. A teacher who teaches a group of children for only one year has a limited picture of her students' social development. She does not have the same opportunity to know her students and to help them grow. Some teachers, however, view the extended time spent with a student in a multiage class as being risky. A dubious colleague asked recently, "What do you do if you get one of those kids that you just don't 'click' with? Isn't it awful to be stuck with a child like that for three or four years?" At first, her questions sounded like logical concerns. Most teachers will admit to those few students in their careers who caused them to count the days until the end of the year. Fortunately, since we have been teaching our multiage class, we have not experienced that particular anguish.

We believe that multiage teachers are forced to look differently at their students from the onset. Again, we compare the idea of multiage grouping to a family grouping. We *are* "stuck" with these students, just as we are "stuck" with our own sons and daughters. All children can be aggravating, rebellious, naughty, you name it, at times. But no matter how they are acting, we love them just the same. And knowing that they are "ours," whether our own offspring or our students for the next three or four years, causes us to work hard to help them to become more caring people. With all our hearts we must invest our time and energy into building relationships with children that work over the long term. We cannot go into a year with the mindset that we will "get through it," and then, whew!, this or that difficult child will move on and become some other poor teacher's responsibility. Instead, it feels good to know that in a multiage class there is time to make a difference.

Even with this luxury of time we find that our work toward creating a caring, responsible community is never done. We attended a two-day conference recently, leaving the children with two substitute teachers. At circle time on our first day back, we asked the children how their days had been. We were surprised at the response to this innocent question: sealed lips and round, wary eyes on all the faces turned toward us. Finally, Lewis put up a tentative hand and blurted out, "We did everything the teachers told us to do."

"Hmm. . . ," we nodded, waiting for more. A few children were squirming.

Finally, five-year-old Benny spoke up, "We had some hard times, because the teacher couldn't look at the plans on her clipboard and watch us at the same time."

"We weren't really helping each other very much," Serene added. More silence. Most of the children were looking at their hands now.

"Well, how about if you tell us about your best times while we were gone," we suggested.

"Math time was good for me, because it was pretty quiet then," Leslie offered.

"Oh, it had been kind of noisy before math?"

"*Really* noisy during Message," Leslie affirmed emphatically.

"My best time was at recess, when we stayed in to clean up the room. We washed the tables." Lewis rolled his eyes. "Rebecca got kind of carried away with the soap." Several children tittered.

As we unraveled other events of those unfortunate days, we became more and more depressed. What had happened to our trustworthy community? Where were the intrinsic, ingrained values? The children voiced one troublesome phrase often, "They let us do it." In our minds this attitude was the root of the problem. Finally, we maneuvered the talk around to a discussion of this question: How can we care for each other and ourselves even when Jane and Penny are not at school? Many good ideas were forthcoming, and we could only take heart in knowing that the children knew how to act even if they hadn't followed through in our absence. We could also hope that the spree of irresponsible behavior had proved to be unpleasant enough to avoid in the future. Little Benny ended the discussion, "We can pray that things will go better next time." We must do more than pray, we thought to ourselves. Once again, we were struck with the realization that community interactions are very fragile. We need to continually make children aware of the power they have to direct their *own* actions.

Behavior is everyone's responsibility in our classrooms. It is not up to us to control children. If we do that, we take away their power to control themselves. Instead, our job is to control the environment in which we put them. We believe that happy kids usually behave. Our job as teachers is to make it *easy* for them to behave by doing everything possible to ensure the happiness of the students while they are at school. We work hard to keep the environment safe, successful, and fun. We work toward providing this secure, happy environment as we create a user-friendly daily schedule and as we show our students that they are valued members of our community.

Establishing a comfortable daily routine is elemental in providing for children's happiness. We have found that our students thrive on a mixture of predictability and choice. We spend much time before school begins in the fall working out the intricacies of the "perfect" daily schedule. We lobby very hard for our special classes (gym, music, and art) to be at a consistent time each day. That done, we can schedule things like Library and Computer during that same time for the days that we don't have a special. With the special classes blocked out in this way, we then structure our days around the long, uninterrupted time spans of our Investigations, Math, and Communications Workshops. The workshops give children the frameworks within which they can make meaningful choices for themselves—choices about things like what they will read and write, how they will extend their literacy in authentic ways, what research group they will get into, what method they will use to solve a math problem, what directions our theme studies will take, and so on. The children can count on their workshops occurring at predictable times; they can count on making choices many times during their week, as well.

Another consideration in our scheduling is to intersperse the sitting, listening times among the hands-on, doing, talking times. Because we are dealing with a multiage group this consideration is close to the surface. The body language of most of our younger children will tell us without a doubt when they have had enough of a sedate, receptive activity. Their antsyness spells relief for our older children, as well, who might exhibit more restraint even though they are not feeling it. All primary age children need to have the opportunities for frequent movement. That is why Investigations Workshop, which is usually an interactive, doing time follows Morning Message, which is a sit quietly, raise your hand to speak, listen to others time. It's why quiet reading follows the frenetic craziness of lunch in our big school cafeteria.

By the time we get the *Perfect Daily Schedule* down on paper in the fall we are pretty confident that the year is going to be a piece of cake! Then . . . the children come to school and mess it all up! From the start we are revising the schedule that looked so great on paper. We make discoveries. Oh wow, we have to allow more than five minutes for getting ready for the bus—the children just aren't making it. And, Choice Time must be too long—that's why we find ourselves so haggard by lunchtime. Wait a minute, we're not giving the half-day kids enough opportunities to read books and to write—we need to incorporate more literacy activities into Investigations Workshop. So we figure out some of the problems ourselves and the kids tell us the rest, and we tinker away on the schedule from Day One. The schedule is never set in stone; it exists to be modified.

Setting up a humane structure for the day is one way we can make it easy for children to be happy. Another way is by valuing the children and making sure they know they are valued. We show our students that they are valued in many ways. Here are a few examples. When we ask for ideas for activities we could do together to support our learning about mammals, children know that their input into the curriculum is important. When we ourselves write in day books, make animals for the habitat mural, or struggle with a math problem, the students see that work in school is significant enough for even adults to do. When we talk with students to set their own literacy goals, they see that we respect their judgment about their learning. When we give honest praise for students' actions and work and thinking, they know that we are sincere because they are proud of these accomplishments themselves. When we allow them to work out their own social problems, they learn that they are capable of mature interactions. When we give them choices about their learning, they recognize that we honor people's different interests and needs. When we challenge any put-down or instance of unkindness, they feel safe.

Children who know that their ideas and feelings are valued are likely to value themselves. They are likely to feel secure enough to care for others. Individual feelings of self-worth and security are the foundation of an effective community. By valuing our students and understanding their needs we are always working toward making our community a better and better place to go to school.

Valuing Learning

While we establish the mechanics of daily procedures and work on the philosophical issue of "how we act in here," we also must concentrate on other needs of our community. These needs are ongoing requirements: that we are learning and that we are valuing that learning. For us, valuing learning leads to more learning.

"What work did you do today that you value?" I ask the children at our end of the day circle.

"What's *value* mean?" Barry wants to know. We can always count on Barry to ask when he needs something cleared up.

We talk about it. Chester says value means *treasure*. "Like what you did today that you *treasure*."

Serene adds, "It's what you did a good job on."

Barry is satisfied with these clarifications. He nods his understanding, and children begin to respond to the question.

"Well," Heidi says smugly, "I read almost the whole book on hamsters." She is obviously pleased with herself. Heidi's forays into nonfiction have been hesitant. Though very comfortable with picture books, she hasn't known she could read well enough to tackle one of the books on the science shelf. Maybe the birth of ten hamster babies on Monday has been a motivator!

Chester comments, "I wrote a lot in my day book about my soccer team." I note that Chester is following through on a Communications Workshop goal he had set on Tuesday: "I will work on writing more details, so I won't have to tell about everything out loud later." I had been impressed with Chester's writing today, too. He had elaborated on paper, rather than orally filling us in with all the details at sharing time. I was glad that Chester was putting more energy into his writing. He really didn't need extra practice talking; he is very good at that already.

Eric is slowly raising his hand. He reports in a surprised voice, "I read one Magic School Bus book and started another one." Eric's goal this week had been to *read* books at quiet reading time, rather than to just *look* at them. Eric is an avid information gatherer; now he is seeing that he can learn even more by reading words in addition to pictures. Eric shakes his head, "I didn't know I could read *that* much."

The children continue their talk about valuing, as I write hurriedly. I want to make sure I get their words down accurately, so that I can transcribe their responses into the End-of-the-Day Questions book. I am impressed with the children's thoughtful answers today. They are showing me that they are serious learners. They have reflected on their needs and set goals for themselves to address those needs. Today they are making discoveries about themselves as learners. They are realizing that they are taking risks or writing better or reading more. They are "treasuring" their own accomplishments and their growth.

As the story about this End-of-the-Day Question session shows, we try to raise self-valuing to a conscious level. By providing the time for reflection, we show children that we want them to think about their actions, their ideas, and their strategies for learning. By giving them opportunities to share their responses to questions, we allow them to experience other perspectives on learning and caring. By writing down their comments, we make them understand that their thoughts are worth recording for future reference. Our questions range from broad ones like "What good thinking did you do today?" to specific ones like "What would be a good topic of conversation to talk about with the guests at your table at our friendship breakfast tomorrow?" Sometimes we think of the question ahead of time and write it up on the board in the morning. Other times we ask the children to suggest a question when we assemble at the end of the day. We are diligent about transferring the responses to the End-of-the-Day Question book each day. These books are well-read. We include a partial list of our End-of-the-Day Questions in Appendix D.

We provide the children in our multiage classes with many such opportunities to think and to talk about their own learning. At other times during the day children identify strategies they are using. They talk about the personal goals they have set. They reflect on how their work is progressing. They metacognate. By devoting so much time to thinking about learning, talking about learning, and listening to others talk about their learning we show children how much we ourselves value the learning process. On the other hand, we believe that a large part of evaluation of learning must come from the students themselves. Over time, they discover how *they* value their own learning. Here are some of the ways the children make it happen in our multiage group.

We ask children to think about their learning strategies regularly during the daily Morning Message. Because we do the message as a whole group activity, one of us is conducting the lesson while the other is observing the children. This system gives us many opportunities to point out good strategies that we notice the children using. A different child each day observes the children during message time, as well. Here's how it all works.

As the message lesson progresses, the teacher and child observers write down on Post-its positive behaviors that they notice in individual children. The teacher is also using a message checklist to keep track of the listening and contributions of six or seven children each day (see Appendix A). As the lesson concludes, the leader asks what the observers have noticed. At this point everyone's ears are tuned and every eye is directed toward the observers' table. This day, just turned six-year-old Hollis reads from the string of Post-its in front of him. "I noticed that Tracy paid attention to the message even though Dan was trying to talk to him. I saw Krista move so that she could see the message better. Darcy did good sound spelling to spell *interesting* on the chart."

The children who have been singled out for recognition are beaming, and it is the teacher observer's turn to comment. Today Jane says, "I was impressed with Chester's summary of the message—he realized that the main idea was in the first sentence of the message this time. I also liked the way Greg knew that the question mark after the last sentence meant that we were *asking* something. Susan explained that she found out how to spell *choice* by finding the word on the Choice Time sign-up sheet. I also saw that Tara, Zack, Nan, Benny, and Sean were actively listening every time I looked at them."

This reporting of observations helps us all become more aware of the learning that is going on at message time. It serves three purposes: the individual child who has been singled out for recognition has an opportunity to reflect on his or her own learning; the other children have been reminded of learning strategies that they might try some day; and all the children have heard more about what we value. And by seeing what we value, they begin to value learning strategies themselves. They become more conscious of their learning. The children know that the comments noted on Post-its will be placed in the class record books, which have separate sections for every child in the multiage class. They know that their accomplishments will not be forgotten.

Children also become more aware of how they value their growth as learners by talking to other students. One afternoon in late January the children were gathered on the rug for a mini-lesson during Communications Workshop. It was an exciting day for the first-year students. It was their first day to stay at school all day. It was their first Communications Workshop, and they were learning about it from their classmates. Serene had the floor right now. She was explaining about day books. She held up her own day book for illustration. "See, you can decorate the cover any way you want. And you can write on a new page every day. Or draw. Be sure to put the date, so you'll remember when you did that page." She paused and said with emphasis, "In your day book you always write about something important to you." She opened her book. "See, here I did this picture and story about my bunnies. On this page I didn't know how to do periods, yet. Now I know about periods. I know lots more than I used to know about writing."

Barry raised his hand to comment. "When you get older you can write more pages, too." He showed his current day-book story. One, two, three, four pages long! We closed the mini-lesson by asking the children to tell about the important thing they were going to write about that day, and they went off to do their writing. Barry and Serene had done their teaching well. The covers of the new day books were elaborately decorated, and important drawings and writings appeared in each one. Not only the newcomers benefited from this mini-lesson, however. Serene's and Barry's reflections on their personal growth as writers had been a catalyst for some of the other older children. Many of them flipped back through their day books that day and considered how their writing had progressed over time. They saw that their day books were valuable records of their growth.

Working with children to set personal literacy goals is another more formal way to concentrate on valuing the learning process. Since literacy goals vary dramatically from child to child in a multiage classroom, we take time to talk with children individually about their goals in goal-review conferences during Communications Workshop. First, in order to see what we will focus on during a conference, we read over the goals the child has been working on in the past two weeks (see Communications Workshop Goals sheet in Appendix E). We then listen to the child read a book he or she wants to share with us. As we listen we take notes on a Post-it, identifying reading strategies the child uses or ignores. Then, we look through the day book together, noting areas of strength and weakness. Finally, we review the student's current goals and help the child set new goals to focus on for the next two- or three-week time period. We talk together about the child's reading and writing, asking for child input on how it's going. We jot down notable information right on the goal-setting sheet. Then it is time to set new goals based on the information we have gathered in this conference. The possibilities are endless. If a child is doing a sketchy job on sound spelling and is having trouble reading his or her day book, a new goal might read: "I will listen and write down all the sounds I hear in a word." If a child is an emergent reader, eager to learn to read books on his or her own, a new goal might read: "I will listen to a story at the listening station at least once a week." Children may have from two to four goals. Usually, the goals are evenly divided between reading and writing goals, between ones the child chooses and ones the teacher suggests.

We just began the formal goal-setting process this year. Though we are still feeling our way along, we are encouraged by results so far. One day in the fall I wrote about goals conferences in my journal:

November 11

I met with Roger a few days ago. He had written about the *Boxcar Children* characters in his day book. I wrote back to him, saying: "Would you like to live in a boxcar? The Boxcar Children are lucky!" He read all the words but *would* and *live*. I told him *would*, hoping that he could then get *live*. He finally did, but it took him a long time. He tried *play* but when I said that that was not the word even though it made sense, he then maintained with a shrug that he didn't know, it was too hard. He kept at it though, reading the words aloud and pausing at the *live*. Finally, he practically shouted, "Live!" He was so proud. We then went on to review Roger's goals and to set new ones. Roger wanted to say that he would write two pages a day in his day book. I persuaded him to modify this goal to "I will write a lot in my day book." At the end of the session, he said, "You didn't have to tell me that word, did you?" For one of our less able readers, he is surprising sometimes. Yesterday, I was sitting writing at the same table with Roger. He wrote a couple of sentences about his new horse, and then announced out loud that he was through writing. I told him that I wasn't, and that he needed to continue to write or draw some more until quiet writing time was over. He chose to write more. When I went to see his work, he had written two pages of big kid writing. He reminded me: "I told you I could write two pages!" Only a short time ago, this zeal to write more would not have been present in our class. Only a couple of kids wrote much or seemed to care much about their writing. The goal setting has helped to increase quantity of writing. I think quality is coming along, too. Both quality of mechanics and of content. We need more authentic audiences, I think, in order to improve quality of content. . . .

I also conferenced with Lisbet. She had done a good job on her capitalization and punctuation goal, but she had not done the reading goal of reading and listing chapter books. I asked her why. She shrugged and said she didn't know. I asked what she had been reading at quiet reading time, because I had noticed how difficult it was for her to put the book down and come to the mini-lesson. She showed me a picture book—quite long and moderately difficult. "I read books like this. By the time I get through with those, it's time to stop." So here was an example of setting a goal that was not appropriate. Though Lisbet could handle the reading level of chapter books, her interest was still in picture books. We changed her goal to "I will read challenging books that I like." She seemed happy. I was glad that she had not felt compelled to work on a goal that she wasn't ready for. I hope others are not feeling pressured to do that. It's such a balancing act.

Our beginning efforts with literacy goals show such promise that in the future we hope to expand the goal-setting format into other areas of learning. Right now goal setting is helping both us and our students to focus on literacy growth. Since we have started setting goals with children we have noticed that they are thinking more about their learning. They have a more evident focus and interest in their work. Typically, one mini-lesson each week is devoted to a round robin sharing of goals, in which each child tells about one current goal and explains why the goal was chosen. By hearing what others are focusing on, children get ideas for directions toward which they might move. We notice, too, that we are more aware of each child's strengths and areas that need attention. The record keeping for this system is painless. The reading notes Post-its go into the class record books, binders containing lined paper and divided into sections for each child. The children keep their goals sheets in their writing folders, each new sheet stapled on top of the others. When the stack gets too big, it goes into the child's portfolio. However, portfolios have a much greater function than merely a place to house records of goals. We are discovering that portfolios are another important element in the valuing of learning process.

Like some other aspects of our multiage program, the development of literacy portfolios is in the fledgling stages. Though portfolios had been on our minds for some time as something we *should* get around to doing, we just didn't seem to get around to doing it during the first three years of our program. Knowing that portfolios were all the rage, we felt a little guilty. We wondered why we did not feel more urgency to evaluate students in this way. We were content with our informal system. We filed our Post-it anecdotal notes away in the class record books, we photocopied representative samples of each child's day-book writing and filed these in folders in the file cabinet, we listened to children read, we questioned them about math strategies, we heard them talk about their ideas, we spoke to each other often about how so-and-so was doing in this or that, we wrote out summaries of student progress, and we had frequent conferences with parents. We watched the children closely; we thought hard about their needs. Really, weren't we doing enough?

It *was* enough from our point of view. However, the children were showing us through goal setting that they were highly involved in the process of their learning. Perhaps creating portfolios would be a good next step for *them*. As graduate students we had found portfolios to be a meaningful way to evaluate our own growth, to combine reflection with representation. Maybe our students needed portfolios to continue the self-valuing process. We decided to ask them.

It was the week before Thanksgiving vacation, and wonders upon wonders, we found ourselves with a little time on our hands. Not wanting to begin a new series of literature groups that would be interrupted by the week-long holiday, we decided to devote that hour each afternoon to exploring the idea of portfolios with the older children. We modeled the process after our work with the University of Maine literacy portfolio development group. On Monday afternoon the children came chattering into the room after recess excited by the smell of popcorn. We got them settled on the floor in front of a huge piece of orange mural paper on the wall and passed out the "thinking food." We asked the children to read and think while they munched. In the center of our large paper was this question: "What do you value about your literacy?"

After a short discussion of what the term *literacy* meant, the children began to give us their value statements. All we had to do was write them down on the big orange paper.

Rebecca spoke first. "I value reading. I can read a lot. Reading helps you to be a better reader."

Other hands were waving. Chester said, "I value my day book, because I can share what I've been learning. Also, when I get older I can look back and see what I did as a kid."

"Yeah," Barry added. "I wrote a story about my two kittens. They sleep on my bed."

After a few more children talked enthusiastically about their day-book writings, Jeff spoke up. "I value Investigations Workshop. It's a time to learn, and then I get to write in my Investigations Log."

Eric was next. "I like Literature Groups. We get to listen to stories and read stories."

Lisbet added, "We get to read stories about God at Sunday School."

The talk went on and on. Thomas said, "I value my homework. It helps me learn to do handwriting and how to spell words. I also value the books that I write. I write about my life or some science things I know."

The paper was filling up. Lewis had one last comment. "I value my imagination. It gives me time to not be in the real world."

The popcorn was gone, the orange paper was full, and dismissal time was near. We closed the session feeling pretty confident that the children would be very interested in creating portfolios to house examples of their valued work. We would talk more about it tomorrow.

The portfolio development sessions the rest of that week were exciting and productive. We began on Tuesday by showing the children our portfolios. We talked about having done the "valuing literacy" exercise with our own classmates at the University. We asked them if they would like to create portfolios. Of course they would! What could they put in them? We worked in small groups and then came together as a whole to determine possibilities for a literacy portfolio. Here is our list:

- Photocopies of favorite stories we have written about important things
- Titles of favorite books we can read or like to listen to
- Math papers
- Reading tests
- Communications Workshop goals
- Tapes of us reading
- Illustrations
- Blue spelling cards
- Book reviews from our literature logs
- Poems we have written
- Personal information and photographs
- Favorite books

Children, teachers, and literature group leaders all had input into this list, and we voted to make final decisions. We were surprised by some of the choices. "Why math papers?" we questioned. The children explained that words are very important when you do math—both written down words, as in word problems and directions on math papers, and words for talking about how you figured something out in math. No problem with that logic, we agreed. We also wondered why they wanted to include the blue spelling cards. These oaktag cards are alphabetical lists of frequently used words. The children keep them in their writing folders and sometimes refer to them to find out how to spell common words when they are writing. We were surprised that they valued these cards, and, besides, we did not consider them to be samples of personal literacy. The children disagreed. "We'll put the cards in at the end of the year to show all the words we can read and find out how to spell. Also, sometimes we write words on there that we use a lot." Okay, we were outvoted on that item. The children were also insistent about putting actual copies of favorite books in their portfolios. We argued that if books were in the portfolios, they would not be available to be read. "Well," the children said, "Maybe we could bring in books from home, and these books wouldn't have to stay in there *all* the time, just for awhile." Okay again. Jane and I lobbied hard for inclusion of photo-copies of representative pages from the day books. We thought that the first couple entries and the last few from each day book would be a good record of growth in writing. This idea was overwhelmingly voted down. The children wanted the portfolio to contain only their favorite writings. They could look at their day books when they wanted to see changes in their writing. If we wanted to copy the day-book pages and keep them somewhere else, that was fine. We had their permission. We decided that it would be fine for these copies to go into the pocket folders in the class record books. No problem.

We were gratified to see how the children took ownership of their portfolios. Knowing that we did not ourselves need the portfolios for evaluation purposes, we were happy to allow the children to assume control of the contents of portfolios. From the outset, we had made it clear that these portfolios would belong to them. We were happy to see that they knew what they valued about their literacy and that they were able to defend their values. In these past few months the children have excitedly added materials to the fat hanging file folders that house their current portfolios. We are glad we took this next step in valuing learn-ing. It has been fun to see the children's joy in their accomplishments.

We know that our work with portfolios in not done. Our exploration process is just beginning. We still have many questions and ideas. We plan to look over our list of portfolio possibilities with the children reg-ularly to see if they want to make deletions or additions. We understand that portfolio structures vary widely, and that portfolios are used for a variety of purposes in schools. Perhaps our district will adopt portfolio evaluation and create standardized guidelines. For right now, though, it feels good to have those portfolios waiting there in the filing cabinet. They are available whenever the children want to look them over, to add to them, to show them to their parents. For the children, the portfolios represent a formal demonstration of some of the things they can do. For us, the portfolios are a concrete manifestation of what we "just know" about our children as learners.

The learning that happens in a multiage class knows no bounds. We feel comfortable evaluating our students by looking at the work and play that they are engaged in each day; by talking with them, their parents, and with each other about their activities at school; by keeping a few notes on our observations of notable occurrences related to any aspect of their learning. Because our children are with us for several years, we feel that we see the continuum of their growth; the children's spurts, their plateaus, and their regressions become evident when we have a long enough time to simply *be* with them, to watch them. We also appreciate this luxury of time as we work with the children's parents. We want to know our parents well; we want them to know us well. Parent/teacher associations that continue uninterrupted for a number of years make it possible to achieve a closeness that is not possible in a single-grade teaching situation. Over time we begin to establish real communication.

Parents feel welcome in our classrooms. They are an integral part of special events and of the daily goings-on. We talk with parents informally often on the phone and in the classroom as they are volunteering or picking up and delivering their children. More formal discussions happen twice a year in scheduled conferences. Near the end of October we begin a round of conferences that takes us up to Thanksgiving. By seeing only two or three parents a week before or after school, we can be leisurely in our talk.

At the conference we discuss the two "formal" reporting-to-parents tools that we use. One is a five-page progress report checklist (see Appendix F), containing a melange of student behaviors, skills, and attitudes. On this report we assign a number, 1, 2, 3, or 4, or NA, to each of the items on this list in an exhaustive attempt to rank students on their *effort* in school. The other document is simpler. It has three sections: one for student comments, one for parent comments, and one for teacher comments (see Appendix G). At conference time the teacher comments section is already filled in (and usually spilling over onto the back of the paper) with information in narrative form about the student's progress. Guess which one of these documents the parents look at first! Invariably, parents will first choose to read about the successes, foibles, strengths, and weaknesses of their child in real words, real sentences, real paragraphs. The conference notes become a starting point for our talk. A half-hour, forty-five minutes, or an hour later we all feel satisfied that we have *communicated* about the child's education. We have looked at the child's math folder, perused the day book, studied the Investigations Log and Literature Log, and looked through the portfolio. We've shared experiences from home and school; we've laughed and sometimes cried together. The conference notes will go home with the parents. At home the student and the parents will write their comments and return the form to school. We'll make a copy to put in the child's section of the class record book and send the original back home. Oops, very often we find we never even get around to discussing the *progress report*!

Since we are required by our district to send home a quarterly assessment of student progress, we designed this progress report specifically for the primary multiage class. In it we attempted to encompass everything we would ever want to say about a child in his or her entire multiage experience with us. We wanted the categories to be open-ended, nonjudgmental, meaningful. We thought we had done it! The document looked great until we tried to use it the first time. Now we realize that it has many drawbacks. It's big, but it doesn't have everything on there we want to say. Someday we intend to revise this monstrosity, but we are not hopeful that the results will be any better. Plain and simple talk works much better.

"Just knowing" and communicating what we know to parents and to the students themselves has worked for us in our evaluation of students for a long time. Unfortunately, "just knowing" does not seem to be enough for our society. Society feels a need to specify in quantifiable terms just how one student compares to another. And schools respond to this need by grading students, by rank ordering them, by testing them on standardized tests. These methods have become accepted as indicators of student progress and motivators for their learning. The results of such methods are accepted as judgments of the quality of students, of schools, and of school districts. They establish a basis of comparison that undermines the value of education. Often we feel like oddballs when we insist that there is no place for competition in learning. Sometimes colleagues argue with us, "Competition is real life! It's what our society is based on." Right, we think. And that is why our society is so messed up!

We exult when we see learning mattering to kids. All of our children come to us caring about learning; it is our job to *keep* them caring about it. Caring about learning is all they really need in order to be learners the rest of their lives. We can help our students to see the merits in their work, but we can't value it for them. Motivation to learn must come from within. Just as we have no wish to be authority figures who regulate the behavior of our students, we do not want to control their academic programs. Children must have choices about their learning. Our aspirations for our students as learners are broad: that they can communicate well with others; that they are interested in solving problems;

that they have a social conscience; and, most importantly, that they value learning. Because we teach in a public school and are bound by a district-mandated curriculum and by district-mandated assessment measures, we are somewhat constrained in our interpretations of how to fulfill these goals. However, we do the best we can within the system and acknowledge that we haven't fought all of our battles yet!

References

COLE, JOANNA. 1989. *The Magic School Bus Inside the Human Body*. New York: Scholastic.

WARNER, GERTRUDE CHANDLER. 1950. *The Boxcar Children*. Chicago: Scott, Foresman.

The Little Room

5

Jane Doan

"10, 9, 8, 7, 6, 5, 4, 3, 2, 1, 0, BLAST OFF!" The children outside the space shuttle shout the countdown. Inside the shuttle, the "space suited" astronauts lean back into their seats as the force of the liftoff pushes them down. Once free of the confines of gravity, they begin their missions. The first experiment, constructing a block stairway and testing the effects of zero-gravity on their Slinky takes intense concentration. Pat records their predictions and results in the ship's "star log." Following this challenging work the crew decides it is time for a snack break. Zero-gravity again poses a problem. Serene almost loses the bag of bread as it floats from her hand. With Tracy's help she holds the bread down, extracts a piece, and spreads it with peanut butter. Pat has similar troubles with the Tang. His problems result in a large spill and a frantic call to mission control requesting instructions on what to do. He flicks the lights five times, the emergency signal, and shouts in a panicked voice, "The Tang is going all over the place!"

"Well, you can't return to Earth for a piddlin' little reason like that. Figure out what to do," is the calm reply from Penny in the control tower. The astronauts succeed at capturing the spill with paper towels. Finally, the snack is eaten and cleaned up. The astronauts get back to work recording the effects of zero-gravity on the ants they have taken with them, photographing the earth they have left behind, and writing down all their observations in the log. Forty-five minutes later they make a safe landing back into our classroom and report the details of their mission to their peers.

The space shuttle trip demonstrates the distance that dramatic play has come in our multiage program. When our program started, the play area was relegated to a small corner of a classroom, an area that offered little creative stimulation. Gradually, as we came to understand the possibilities provided by an exciting space that encouraged authentic play, the area grew and changed. This chapter offers a short history of these changes.

Dramatic play began in our multiage classroom as a way to offer the children an opportunity to use their imaginations to extend the current theme study. We believed that engaging in creative activities that related to the knowledge they were accumulating would help them to retain that knowledge. When we began encouraging dramatic play, we did not suspect how important it would become to our program.

Early role-playing situations in our class were sporadic and were casually organized in a corner of a classroom, usually Penny's. The first designated space was "the dump" that grew out of our study of *The Boxcar Children*. The students were intrigued by the dump in that book where the characters found many articles to recycle into things they needed. "We could have our own dump to recycle stuff," they suggested. And they set about providing us with one. The students supplied the dump with empty milk cartons, scraps of paper, pieces of wire, gum wrappers, straws, and other assorted treasures they found at home. These treasures were placed in a large box in Penny's room, and all the children were free to scavenge in the dump. The children used the dump frequently and made many fanciful and useful articles. The dump was maintained entirely by student contributions. The children insisted on reviving the dump the next fall, and they continued to find uses for it throughout that school year.

The next dramatic play area was developed as a way to incorporate handwriting practice into a real-life situation. During our colors theme, we created a sign shop, also located in a corner of Penny's room. The children made up an order form, which they distributed to the secretaries, other teachers, and principals in our school, and to their families. The response was enthusiastic. As the orders came in the children used various art materials to make the requested signs. Soon signs designed and painted by our students were decorating the halls and classrooms of our school. The sign shop seemed to fill a need for others as well as for our students. We were able to perform a service for our school and our families. One sign, "Phoebe's Room," was ordered by Penny's daughter and still hangs on the door of her bedroom. The children had found a useful and meaningful way to practice their handwriting, make patterns, and learn about mixing colors.

Another teacher-initiated area was related to our construction theme. We had begun to collect a few props. When we put these items out for the students to use, we saw how wearing hard hats, calling contractors on a real phone, and making blueprints stimulated their play. Once again, our dramatic play area was located in Penny's room. In the construction office the children accepted orders for constructions, drew up their blueprints on graph paper, and used various materials to build houses, factories, and cities. Their imaginative constructions were displayed for all their peers to see.

These three areas were much like learning centers. The children chose whether or not to go to them. Not all the children participated. The dramatic play was limited because these spaces were product oriented. They were located in a corner of one of our rooms, a space too small and open to allow for much uninhibited dramatic play. We were aware of the limitations of the dramatic play areas, but we were not sure how to make them more successful.

In the third year of our multiage program we expanded on the idea of a dramatic play area. Because we had noticed how involved children become in their learning when they see real purposes for it, we wanted our dramatic play area to more closely simulate real-life situations.

Between our classrooms there is a small room that we used primarily as a passageway. It is six feet by eight feet and has a built-in table along one wall and a small trapezoid table on the opposite wall. We realized that this room was a space that could be revamped as our theme changed. It gave us a space that could be made to imitate a real-life site. It also offered a self-contained area that was relatively private, giving the children the opportunity to use their imaginations without feeling that they were being observed by the teachers and the other children.

The Little Room became incorporated into our theme studies gradually. We first used it as a cave during our rock theme. The children enjoyed covering the walls with construction paper rocks. Walking through the cave from one room to the other soon became a favorite activity. However, the cave was just a cave, a dark and exciting passageway. Perhaps it stimulated the children's imaginations, allowing them to visualize bats or bears, but we still had not recognized its possibilities as a stage for dramatic play.

When we began to study astronomy we decided to have the children decorate the Little Room as a space shuttle. The shuttle *Discovery* was in orbit at that time and the children were excited by the idea. At our direction, they created computers to run the ship, cameras to photograph the sights, and other realistic-looking buttons and knobs to represent controls. The older children quickly educated the younger ones about just what a shuttle needed in order to be functional. Penny and I devised the four missions and collected the materials the children were to use. We also included a small library of space books to be read if any of the astronauts had the leisure time to do so. The children were asked with whom they would like to travel on a space shuttle, and we used this information to create multiage groups of four children who together would enter the shuttle for forty-five-minute periods. The effect the shuttle had on the students amazed us. The younger children quickly reintroduced the older children to the world of the imagination. The older children directed the play toward authenticity.

"We are in space now. If you look out the window, the earth will look like a blue ball wrapped in white clouds," Thomas sagely advises Chester. "Earth is not flat like it looks when we are standing on it. It just looks that way because it is so big. It really is round. Honest!"

"How can you be sure? It looks flat to me," says Chester.

"Thomas is right. He really is," pipes up Miranda. "You can believe him because I have seen pictures on TV that the real space shuttle has sent back to earth."

All the children used and extended the information they were learning about the stars and the planets. The children loved the shuttle. Even though the activities were mainly teacher directed, the children found time to allow their imaginations free rein, and dramatic play achieved a new status in our curriculum.

Since the space shuttle had been so successful, we eagerly planned to use the Little Room with each theme. During our next theme study, weather, the Little Room was turned into a weather station. Once again, the teachers decided not only what the Little Room would become, but also the activities that the children would be asked to do during their stay in the weather station. Colby College in Waterville, Maine, had loaned us real weather instruments to measure temperature, wind velocity, wind direction, and barometric pressure. Penny and I filled the room with weather charts and posters, and a large supply of books about the weather. Forms for filling in the accrued weather data were also included. To our dismay the children did not seem to enjoy being meteorologists. Or perhaps they felt that the weather station was just another teacher-directed activity that they had to do. They were unsure what a weather person did, what function a weather station performed. It was not real to them. A weather person was someone on the television. Probably, we would have been better off if we had turned the Little Room into a TV studio instead.

We learned from our experiences with the weather station that the success of dramatic play depended on the extent of the children's background knowledge. In order for them to use their knowledge, they needed to assume more control of the Little Room. If it was to be their space, the children should be the ones to decide what the room would become. Then they should be in charge of creating the environment.

At the beginning of our pet theme the class brainstormed ideas for what the Little Room could become.

"I want it to be a doghouse. I love my dog," stated Sasha.

"But I love my horse," cried out Casey. "I want it to be a stable. We could make pretend horses and groom them and ride them and even have horse shows!"

"If it were a pet zoo, we could have all different kinds of animals," put in our class appeaser, Serena.

"I know! I know!" exclaimed Roger. "We could have it be a veterinary hospital and our pets could go there when they are sick or hurt. We could be the pet owners and some of us could be vets."

"That would be awesome," agreed Justin.

Following much more animated discussion, the children voted to turn the Little Room into a veterinary hospital. Suddenly it turned out that many of the children had ailing pets at home. Penny and the children worked together during a whole week at Investigations Time to transform the space into a hospital for their stuffed animals. After much discussion of what equipment a veterinarian's hospital would need they worked in small groups to make X-rays of various animals, and develop medicines and veterinary tools. They also created currency and set their own fees. A waiting-room area was set up outside the Little Room, complete with magazines and forms to fill out. The shelves of the classroom museum were filled with sick and maimed toy animals waiting for appointments. Hoping that some math would occur, Penny and I added scales and measuring tapes to the hospital setup. Once again, the children worked in the Little Room in multiage groups of four. After their forty-five minutes of being vets and/or pet owners, they shared their experiences with the rest of the class. The children were enthusiastic about their work in the hospital. The older children acted as directors, setting the play into action. The younger children quickly moved into their roles as vets or owners, and their use of their imaginations spurred the older children into relaxing and using theirs. They were highly involved in setting up and playing in this area because it was very real for them. They understood its function in real life. Their parents also joined in. One day a forlorn stuffed puppy was found outside our door. The envelope taped to his back contained a red felt tongue and the question "Do you perform glue surgery?" Of course our vets did!

Life long ago was our next theme. Again, we asked the children what they would like the Little Room to become. Remembering our visit to the 1850's school house at the Norlands Farm, the children were eager to re-enact their experiences there. Of course, the Little Room would become our own old-fashioned schoolhouse. Penny found some old readers and spelling books and offered them to the children to include in their school. During a lengthy class meeting, the children made suggestions about how the school would operate. They found slates, pointers, and quill pens to put in their schoolhouse. After making a craft-paper chalkboard and brown-paper copybooks, they were ready to start. This use of the Little Room took few props. All that was necessary for success was a strict schoolmarm or schoolmaster! The children each took a turn as teacher and "kept" school, as their peers did recitations and seatwork in the tasks of spelling, reading, math, and handwriting.

In our program themes are done on a three-year rotation. When we returned to *The Boxcar Children* as our theme, it inspired the children to have a boxcar where they could become Benny, Violet, Jessie, and Henry. The props needed were few: a cracked cup, a few dishes, and an iron pot. This time all the students readily got into their roles as the Alden children. They spent their time in the boxcar playing imaginatively; we did not direct any of their activities. Though the children had a script of sorts based on the adventures in the book, they went far beyond those adventures, devising all sorts of places for the children to go and things for them to do. Of course, excursions to the "dump" to find usable articles were frequent, and many groups found that the uni-fix cubes could stand for eggs which the Alden children could gather. But the Alden children in our Little Room also made trips through dangerous forests or went to Disney World. Some groups had their adventures with the Mutant Ninja Turtles, combining the newer movie characters with their friends from the world of books.

An animal lab, full of strange scientific tools, animal track rubbings, and a library of mammal books was the next incarnation of the Little Room. This lab became the site of serious learning as the animal researchers each chose an animal to research. The older children helped the younger ones with the reading of texts and the identifying of mammal tracks. As the children shared their experiences with their peers, they also chose whether to display their research in the Little Room or to take it home to share with their parents.

The transformation of the Little Room into the multiage greenhouse was the most successful simulation yet. The activities, as well as the accouterments of the greenhouse, were all devised by the children. Prior to deciding on having a greenhouse we had visited a local greenhouse and had been introduced to the activities that took place there. Once again, a week of careful preparation was necessary to put the greenhouse together. The children worked cooperatively in multiage groups, sharing ideas and expertise, to design an elaborate greenhouse that even included a sprinkler system. Dramatic play in this area was vivid, both because the children had firsthand knowledge of what went on at a greenhouse and because they had total ownership over this particular greenhouse.

As we listened to the children's talk, we realized that knowledge and imagination are the best combination for satisfying dramatic play.

"I liked singing the song about the bee," stated Lewis.

"What song about a bee?" I asked. None of the other children had mentioned such a song and I was genuinely puzzled.

"Rebecca taught me a song," he said solemnly. "It was when we were being attacked by a swarm of angry bees."

Rebecca chimed in, "We had to turn on all the water to try to get them out. The water was so heavy that the guy that fixes the wires had to come." It seems their stay in the greenhouse was filled with problems, many of which were solved by singing!

Thomas added, "I learned how to plant seeds in there and it helped me learn more about plants. Now, I like learning a lot. I try to get myself as much work as possible so that I can learn more."

"I learned not to put the seeds down in the bottom of the milk carton because then they may not grow!" interrupted Miranda, anxious to share her discovery.

Nan contributed, "When I was in the greenhouse we pretended people were on the phone calling to order flowers. One man wanted 100 roses, 99 pocketbook plants, 10 dandelions, and 5 sunflowers for his girlfriend."

Thomas asked, "How much did those flowers cost?"

"Two thousand dollars!" was her reply.

Leslie interjected, "We pretended Chester really swallowed a cactus. We had to take him to the hospital."

"I told a man that the flowers he wanted were three thousand dollars and he just hung up on me," an amazed Carter stated.

Rebecca looked aghast. "Well, that's way too expensive. No one would pay that much for flowers!"

The Little Room has become one of the favorite places in our classrooms. The children check each morning to see who the horticulturists, veterinarians, or astronauts will be that day during Investigations Workshop. They sign up to use the Little Room during Choice Time and clamor to go in there whenever inclement weather requires us to have an inside recess. When we begin a new theme, the children's first question is, "What can we turn the Little Room into this time?" and the brainstorming begins. The children collaborate on developing their ideas into a creative place where their imaginations can soar. Knowing that the Little Room is theirs in a way that the larger classrooms can never be, they decide what it will look like and what will happen there. The children are limited only by the range of their inspirations.

Dramatic play seems a natural in a multiage classroom. The wide developmental span of the children creates a stimulating environment for creative thinking. The nurturing nature of the older students, when combined with the openness of the younger students, leads to dramatic play that benefits all the age levels.

As pleased as we are with the Little Room as a dramatic play area, we still see that improvements can be made. We plan to allow more student selection of the groupings. We will encourage even more student autonomy in deciding what the room will look like and what activities will be pursued there. Each group will be expected to decide on a way to demonstrate to the rest of the class what they experienced in the Little Room. As we use the children's ideas to make improvements in the Little Room concept, we will allow it to become their own vision.

References

Warner, Gertrude Chandler. 1950. *The Boxcar Children*. Chicago: Scott, Foresman.

The Pumpkin Project

6

Penelle Chase

My driveway was already lined with cars and more were coming. The children, along with assorted brothers and sisters and parents, were spilling out onto the lawn, hoes and bug spray in hand. Jane and I breathed a sigh of relief. The storm front had gone through to our south, leaving us with a clear midsummer evening, a perfect night for our second weeding party. School had been out for almost a month; we were glad that so many of our students were rolling in for this half-work, half-social occasion. Barry raced up to us, legs and arms churning, body upright, in his unique running style. "Penny! Jane! Guess what?" He stood before us, hands on hips, dazzling us, as usual, with his charm.

How else could we respond? "What, Barry?"

"I'm six now! I had my birthday on June 15! Did you see how fast I ran over here?"

"We noticed that!" Jane said. "You've gotten a lot faster recently! Are you ready to pull lots of weeds in the pumpkin patch?" His vigorous nods were meant to convince us. I gave Jane a "we'll see" look, and she rolled her eyes at me.

"Should we get these folks organized?" I asked her.

"We better," she laughed. "Before the bugs get too bad. You're the farmer! You talk to them!"

The group did not need much direction. The children knew the way to the pumpkin patch. In May they had all helped plant the pumpkin seeds, cutting slits to make *X*'s in the black plastic at two-foot intervals, folding back the plastic to make little square openings, and pushing three seeds "just an inch deep" into the soil. They had worked carefully. The older children had also planted last year; they had cautioned the new planters about putting the seeds in too deep: "We want these seeds to come up!" Many of their parents had helped on planting day, too. And many of those parents had returned to the farm in late June, bringing their children to tend the pumpkins, to thin them to two plants per hole, to pull the tiny weeds coming up along the edges of the plastic. Now two rows of pumpkins, each row 150 feet long and covered with a filmy netting to keep the young plants warm and bug-free, awaited inspection. Everyone was anxious to see how the plants were growing.

"We have two jobs to do tonight," I began to speak to the crowd. "We need to take off the row cover and fold it up carefully, so we can use it again next year. And we need to pull up the weeds that have grown along the sides of the plastic. We can head to the field now. But before anyone starts working, there is one plant out there I'd like you to look at. It's different from all the others, much smaller. I bet you'll be able to figure out why when you see it!"

When we got to the field, I showed some of the children the stunted pumpkin plant at the end of one of our rows. I had predicted correctly. Several of the children figured out right away that the small pumpkin plant had somehow been left uncovered by the netting and had not benefited from the captured warmth that had caused the others to grow so rampantly. The plants were bursting at the seams, pushing against the row cover, which was secured by rocks along the edges. We all "oohed" and "aahed" as we peeled back the covering and began weeding. Barry worked hard for perhaps five minutes before he straightened up with a sigh and commented sagely, "I guess I better stop. I've got back trouble, you know."

Elizabeth, Serene's older sister and a graduate of our class, smiled indulgently at this announcement and said, "Maybe you should take a break, Barry." With so many weeders, the work was finished quickly. Barry, along with a few others, stayed happily on break until we were heading down the road back to the house, at which point he gained a sudden burst of energy and tore off. I commented to his mom who was walking with me, "I *thought* six was kind of young for back trouble."

She laughed. "He's ready for that picnic supper I packed. Food and fun cure all Barry's ills!"

We picnicked on the lawn, the children played, the adults chatted. As dark fell, parents herded the children, still going strong, back into the cars. Another successful weeding event was over, and the pumpkins were on their own now until we harvested them before the first September frost. As I walked Jane to her car she asked, "Did you notice Jeff tonight? When he first got here he looked around and made a disgruntled comment about how 'not many big kids are here.' But later, even after more of the older kids had shown up, he was interacting mostly with the new children, showing them what to do in the pumpkin patch, getting them involved in games on the lawn. Even his mother commented on how great it was to see him having grown into his new role as one of the older kids."

I nodded. "We are privileged, you know, to get to watch these children change over the years. Never mind years, though! I was amazed at how much Darcy has grown up in just a month. She was weeding near me and I pointed out that the pumpkins had buds on them. Right away she said, 'Oh, we got the row cover off just in time, didn't we!' I was surprised; she had remembered our discussion in the spring about the bees needing to be able to get to the flowers to pollinate them."

Jane nodded. "We've seen it over and over in this pumpkin project! When children are doing something real, they learn without even realizing they're learning. This is the way school should be all the time." Jane waved good-bye and headed down the drive.

Jane was right. The pumpkin project had become a very important part of our multiage program. It had everything! All the essential elements for meaningful education were embodied in growing and marketing these pumpkins. The project allowed for the integration of learnings from every subject area. It provided real work for real reasons. It involved parents and siblings. Best of all, it was an ongoing project that followed the cycle of the seasons, rather than the school calendar. It was the absolute coming together of our ideas on multiage learning.

We started raising pumpkins for fun and profit in the spring of 1991. We had applied for funds from the Western Maine Partnership out of the University of Maine at Farmington, and we were awarded $270 for our grant entitled "Seed Money." Originally, our primary motivation was monetary. School funding was very tight at that time; all non-necessities were being stripped from school budgets. A year without field trips was looking pretty bleak. Our plan was simple. The "seed money" would provide our class with the resources to raise pumpkins on my farm, and we would sell the pumpkins at our school in the fall. We would use the proceeds from the sale to finance a trip to the Norlands Living History Center the following spring. We had always wanted to go there in connection with our study of "Life Long Ago," but we had never been able to afford it. However, necessity is the mother of invention, and we knew that we had been successful writing grants in the past. We decided to apply. The application form was short and straightforward. We settled down at my house on a Saturday afternoon in January to tackle it. "This first question looks easy enough," we thought.

1. Indicate the grade(s) in which your project will be used and approximate number of students who will benefit.

"There are thirty-six children in our combined classes, ranging in age from five to eight years old." We wrote that down and then stopped to consider. That will be the number of children who actually harvest and sell the pumpkins. But, many more children will benefit. Our graduates will have helped with the ordering of supplies and the planting in the spring. Some of them will have come out with their families to weed pumpkins in the summer. And we will invite them to join us when we take our big trip to the Norlands Farm. But, talking about benefits, what about teacher benefits? We will get to reap the final reward along with the children, as well as benefit by learning the ins and outs of pumpkin production. Benefits in school shouldn't be reserved just for kids, we reasoned. Adults are learners, too. The parents of our students had shown us that time after time as they became involved with our themes and helped in our classrooms. Knowing them, we believed they would flock to the farm to help us in every stage of this pumpkin project. They would be on hand on the day that we distributed pumpkins to all the school children who had placed orders. We could already see pictures in our minds of satisfied young customers lugging pumpkins back to their classrooms. Since pumpkins make just about everybody happy, we guessed that folks of all ages would benefit! On to the next question.

2. State the subject or curriculum area toward which your project will be directed. If project is interdisciplinary, name dominant subject area.

Another easy one. Well, we figured, planting stuff has got to be considered science. We'll study all about the soil and the parts of a seed and the functions of the different parts of a plant. Hmm, some talk about the seasons would surely relate, as well, since we would be planting the pumpkins in the spring, tending them in the summer, and harvesting them in the fall. Great, all these areas so far were right there listed as objectives in our Science Curriculum Guide. Or was seasons in the social studies curriculum? Wait, this project could cover lots of other social studies topics, too. When we got around to marketing the pumpkins, we could delve into basic theories of economics, things such as the concepts of supply and demand, free enterprise, division of labor. Also advertising! We would have to create posters to hang up around school and some flyers to distribute. It would be interesting to get into a study of effective advertising. That might lead into some revelations on consumerism. That would be social studies, too, wouldn't it? Or no, maybe it would fall under thinking skills or life skills, along with learning about how to manage a savings account, which we would certainly want to teach the children. But maybe money issues should be called math. Yes, of course, pricing the pumpkins, keeping an accounting of expenses, making change, counting money, all that number stuff would be considered math. But there were lots of other math topics, too. Important things like learning how to use a scale to weigh the pumpkins, working with a tape measure to distribute the seeds evenly, and figuring out how much space we needed for planting and how many seeds we needed to buy. Or would that kind of figuring be considered problem solving? And we would surely be making some graphs to compare the various sized pumpkins. Interpreting graphs was considered math, too. But comparing is language arts, too. You know, small, medium, and large, big, bigger, biggest. Those concepts would be pretty easy to grasp if you were sorting pumpkins into piles. Come to think of it, we would have occasion to use lots of language in this project. We would be talking and listening to each other as we worked and made decisions. Talking and listening are important elements in a language arts curriculum. And in addition to oral language, we would be doing lots of actual reading and writing as we made charts, did research, created posters and signs, and enjoyed pumpkin literature. Whew, the possibilities were endless! But what should we put down for our *dominant subject area*?

"How about horticulture," my husband, Addison, who is really the farmer, suggested. "The children will be learning a lot about plant husbandry, really. And about plastic mulch, row covers, fertilizer, frost protection, storage of pumpkins, all kinds of agricultural information." Horticulture. That sounds pretty comprehensive, we thought, and we shrugged and wrote it down.

3. Indicate the number of students with special needs who will benefit from this project. How will the goals (cognitive and/or affective) benefit students with special needs?

Whoa, these questions brought us up short. Special needs? Why, all of our children had special needs. We avoided separating out certain children and designating them as having needs more special than others. "We have a heterogeneous mixture of children," we wrote. "All thirty-six of them have definite strengths and needs. All children will be fully included in all activities. The project will provide many varied opportunities for children to use cognitive skills in the areas of reading, writing, and math. Students will be actively involved in planning this project, as well as in implementing it. The children will join us in problem solving, making decisions, experimenting, and examining results. There are jobs for everyone in this project—everyone will experience success. Doing real work for real reasons will promote independence and self-esteem." That about covers it, we thought. But we were nervous. The Western Maine Partnership received many of its grants from federal special education funds. Would they agree with our all-inclusive philosophy for dealing with children? In a multiage class the diversity of needs is pronounced, simply because the range of developmental levels is so wide. It becomes second nature to address the individual needs of children, whatever they may be. We invite into the classroom any and all resource people who can help us in meeting the needs of students. Our children stay in the classroom to participate in whatever's going on; they engage in activities that are appropriate for them. Except for the speech therapist's work with individual children on articulation difficulties, and the physical education teacher's intervention with those children having gross motor needs, other specialists work with children within the classroom setting. Instead of removing a child from the classroom and running the risk that the child will feel "specially" deficient, we work at making every child feel special for his or her gifts. We work at providing activities that children can approach and accept at their own individual levels and experience success. We hoped that the Western Maine Partnership would agree with our idea of "specialness." Feeling a little less confident, we went on to the next question.

4. Identify the key student learning activities that will be in your project.

"Haven't we already done this in question #2?" I complained.

"Yes, we did, in a general way, when we identified the key subject area," Jane agreed. "But, let's just brainstorm all the possibilities for activities that we *could* do in connection with this project." We started out tentatively, but we soon gathered steam. The list got longer and longer. In Math we would be:

- filling out seed order forms
- calculating how many seeds to buy
- figuring out space needed for planting
- managing a bank account
- keeping an accounting of expenses
- calculating net profits
- measuring between plants
- weighing pumpkins
- pricing pumpkins
- making change
- counting money.

In social studies we could study:

- seasons of the year
- division of labor

- concept of supply and demand
- concept of free enterprise.

In science we would address these questions:

- What do we need to know about the life cycle of plants?
- Why should we use row cover?
- Why should we use black plastic?
- How much fertilizer do we need?
- How do we store pumpkins?
- How do we protect them from frost?
- How do we read a thermometer?

In language arts we would:

- make graphs
- make charts
- write letters
- read fiction and nonfiction selections
- write fiction and nonfiction
- create posters and signs
- advertise
- learn research skills
- talk and listen to each other.

We would solve problems and make decisions:

- What varieties of pumpkins should we plant?
- How should we advertise?
- How much should we charge?
- How can we divide up the work?
- How can we work together effectively?

"That *must* be it," I announced, as I scanned the list.

But Jane disagreed. "I really think that the possibilities for learnings in this project are endless. The kids will direct the focus of the curriculum as we go along. Each year will be different."

"But certainly this amount of learnings will satisfy the grant-givers," I pleaded.

"Yes, it will. Write it down!"

So we did, still wondering in the backs of our minds what key learning opportunities we had forgotten. This project was getting to be out of control, and we didn't have a single seed in the ground yet!

5. Describe how you will know if your project has made a difference with students and achieved its desired goals.

The afternoon was wearing on. I stood up to stretch and looked out my window at the snow-covered fields reaching away toward the dark trees. How will planting pumpkins in those fields make a difference to kids? How would we know that we had achieved our goals? "Either I'm tired or this is a tiresome question," I thought. "Some things you just *know*," I said to Jane. "Why are educators so hung up on proof?"

I had been dreaming of a pumpkin project like this for a long time. Ever since, when years ago Richard Murray, a neighbor who was more of an entrepreneur than we were, had suggested it to Addison: "You know, you really ought to plant pumpkins in that paddock where you keep the cows all winter. I'll sell them for you and we'll split the profits." Our two daughters, Meg and Phoebe, who were probably six and seven then, entered into this venture with joy. They helped pick the rocks after Addison plowed, they helped plant the seeds, they trailed after me when I rototilled. They discovered the new blossoms and watched as the baby pumpkins developed. As the fruit grew, they waited impatiently for the pumpkins to turn orange. We agonized together when we discovered woodchuck devastation in the middle of the patch. Picking the pumpkins was the occasion for a party. All the neighbor kids were there to help cut the fruits from the vine and load them onto the trailer. The children had their pick of pumpkins for Halloween, and our share of the money that Richard made by selling the pumpkins in town was pure cream. We set that money aside for fun. As parents, we did not need any formal assessment of this pumpkin venture to know how valuable it was for our children. Besides the "scientific" learnings that they gained by growing pumpkins, they had worked cooperatively to accomplish a task. They had shared in the rewards, both tangible and intangible. There was a completeness to the whole process that was *right*. I knew that a pumpkin project would be right for school children, too.

Question #5 was asking us, in a nice way really, to justify the project, to measure its success. We put aside our stubbornness and wrote: "We will ask the children to evaluate the project, to describe their learnings and their feelings about the project. We will survey parents.

Since the new five-year-olds will have had a chance to interact with the older children during summer weeding sessions, we will look for cohesion in our group when school starts in the fall. If the children decide that they want to repeat the project the following year, we will know it has been a success."

6. Indicate approximate time needed to implement and complete this project.

Hey, we liked this question! This project would be a bargain for anyone to fund, because it would be on-going and self-sustaining. We could plant pumpkins in the spring, tend them during the summer, and harvest and sell them in the fall. Using some of the money we earned, we could refinance this process for as long as we chose. This project would follow the cycle of the seasons, rather than be defined by the months of the school year. We liked the continuity of that concept, probably because it reminded us of the cyclical nature of our multiage class. Our class did not *end* when school ended in the spring. Two-thirds of the children were back again in the fall. "When school starts the older ones are there to help tend the new little sprouts," Jane joked. I had to get her back on task. "You are corny, Jane," I reminded her. "Write this down: The initial project will begin in the spring of 1991 and conclude in the fall of 1991. The recovered 'seed money' should enable us to finance another pumpkin planting the following year." Next question, please!

7. Estimate the approximate cost of implementing this project.

Happily, farmers aren't too busy in January. Addison's expertise came in handy for this question. With the Johnny's Selected Seeds catalogue in hand he estimated: "$5.00 for seeds, $20.00 for fertilizer, $25.00 for degradable mulch, $40.00 for floating row cover. That should do it to get them in the ground. Oh, add twenty bucks for gas for the tractor and the truck." That doesn't sound like much, we thought, before we remembered the original reason for this project—to earn money for field trips. Probably we would have to pay for getting the children back and forth to the farm in the spring and fall. "That's another $150 for transportation when you count paying for the bus driver, too," Jane calculated. Adding in ten more dollars for video tapes, our grand total came to $270.00. Like we said, a bargain! With any luck this seed money would be recouped along with plenty of "fun money" left over.

8. Overall value: write a few sentences that "sell" your project.

The last question! We answered it quickly. "Seed money will provide us with the opportunity to engage in real work for real reasons. Learning across the entire curriculum will occur naturally. We will learn as we do, and all of us will experience success. Working cooperatively toward a common goal will foster the development of a strong sense of community among the children, parents, and teachers. The learning journey will be a reward in itself. Getting to go on special trips will be the icing on the cake!"

It had been a long afternoon. This job had been more challenging than we had expected. But, as we folded the application into an envelope, we discovered a new excitement underlying our tiredness. In writing the grant application we began to see glimmers of the possibilities that this project might offer. Maybe there were academic, social, and emotional learnings that exceeded our original mercenary requirements. The application questions had made us think. They had made us probe more deeply into the reasons why we value a multiage framework in schools. And they had made us see that we might really be onto something with this pumpkin scheme that would be a perfect example of multiage education.

True confessions time. We have never done the evaluation piece, which we promised to do in question #5 on the application form. We have not needed to. The pumpkin project has panned out to be everything that we dreamed it could be, and more. Its value is obvious. In a fall journal entry I describe an Investigations Workshop that illustrates the importance of pumpkins in our learning:

September 29

During Investigations today we got organized to sell the pumpkins. We had several different groups going simultaneously—Andrea and Emily, our student teachers, made pumpkin cookies with two groups; Jane worked with a group to decorate a refrigerator box, which will become our pumpkin store. My group was in charge of the order form and the record keeping. It included Carter, Chester, Thomas, Justin, Jeff, Darcy, Nan, and Benny. Before we could even get going, we had to decide if we wanted to change our prices from last year. We had lots of discussion about current economic conditions and how money was scarce. "My parents don't have much money," from Benny. But, since our big pumpkins were bigger, and since we had lots of big pumpkins, the final vote was to raise the price on the big pumpkins and add a category for Baby Bear, the new variety developed by Johnny's Selected Seeds. I threw my opinion out into the discussion arena (I thought we might have trouble selling the pumpkins if we raised our prices), but I was outvoted. When we were ready to vote on the two options we had discussed, I asked if there were any other ideas. One of the five-year-olds went down the line of the pumpkins displayed: "Minis should be fifty cents, Baby Bears a dollar, Smalls two dollars, Mediums twenty cents and Larges five cents." Oh, well, this child has two more years with us. . . . In the end we decided on: Mini—fifty cents; Baby Bear— one dollar; Small—two dollars; Medium—three dollars; Large—four dollars. I hope we can sell the pumpkins for these prices. If not, I guess the kids will have learned a lesson in Real Life. Jeff and Darcy designed a new order form. It's well organized and readable. Jeff did most of the writing. The legibility is surprising—Jeff is often messy. But, I guess writing for real reasons. . . . We also worked on the filing system— putting labels on old folders, putting room numbers on these and then writing the teachers' names below. The children did very well on this— Nan and Carter worked cooperatively, and so did Roger and Thomas— surprising pairs to be so compatible. Maybe when kids are presented with a real job that needs to be done, they know that cooperation is essential. Later, Rebecca, Justin, and Heidi made some tallying forms so we could keep track of what sizes had been sold that day. The kids remembered the problem we had had last year when we didn't know how many of each size we had and didn't keep good track of what we had sold. It's great to have done this process before and have the opportunity to try to improve. Serene and Hannah made price signs to display with the various sizes of pumpkins. Everyone was very productively busy for an hour and fifteen minutes. Heidi's comment was: "I can't believe the morning is over."

Sessions like this one are common when we are doing pumpkin work. The children see their roles and jobs change as they grow and move through the multiage program. Except for a few aching backs at weeding sessions, the children always enter into the work zealously. They could do it all day long and come back the next day ready for more. School *should* be like this more often.

Besides *realness*, the ongoing nature of the pumpkin project is another big key to its success. The continuity of the multiage program allows for it to happen this way. The farming aspect of the project starts in the spring, continues through the summer, and wraps up in the fall. Yet even in the dead of winter we might find ourselves checking out the seed catalogue to see what varieties of pumpkins will be offered this year. Also, winter is a season for enjoying our stash of pumpkin money! We decide together how we will use it. We consider Zack's suggestion that the class go to a restaurant for dinner and decide instead to invite all the adult helpers in the school to be our breakfast guests at a local restaurant. We plan our friendship breakfast for Valentine's Day, and get busy on invitations.

When spring comes and our planning and calculating and ordering are complete, we are ready to plant again. We write letters to the incoming five-year-olds inviting them to join us on planting day. Our students are excited to meet the children who will be new to our class in the fall. We remember planting last year; some of the seeds had been uncovered by a heavy rain. We will be sure to plant them deeply enough this time. Carter remembers last year, too, when he was a new kid. He had knocked over a wheelbarrow, and kids had laughed at him. "Not *at* you, Carter. *With* you." But Carter's painful memory causes us to spend some time talking about how to make the new students feel comfortable among all these strangers. All the time we are learning more about how to do things better. We refine our work. Another growing season is about to begin.

Part Two: Ripples

Widening Circles 7

Penelle Chase and Contributing Educators

The day had come. We had never been so nervous in our lives. Why had we agreed to do this presentation for the Re-Imagining Schools conference? At last count 150 people had signed up for our talk. That put our audience at approximately 125 more than we were used to. Obviously, we were not going to be able to follow our usual format of sitting in a circle, chatting and joking informally with the workshop participants, as we explained our program. We had had no idea what we were getting into when we agreed to do this presentation months ago. If we had been thinking, we should have known that a conference co-sponsored by the University of Maine Literacy Department and The Center for Teaching and Learning, organized by energetic and creative people like Brenda Power, Jan Kristo, and Nancie Atwell, would draw big crowds. But 150 people! "Brenda, you made us sound too good in this conference flyer!" we had accused her earlier that spring.

> Penelle Chase and Jane Doan will show how they have abandoned math, science, social studies, and literacy categories in their multiage, team-taught classroom. These teachers instead segment the day into two workshops, *Investigations* and *Communications*. Penny and Jane will show how this radical restructuring of their day affects both their students and their own perceptions of learning. This workshop is also recommended for teachers interested in multiage classrooms and co-teaching strategies.

"How can we possibly reach that many people and have them understand what we are doing? That would be difficult to do even with a small group in an hour and fifteen minutes!"

Brenda's response was her usual one. She laughed. "You'll be fine! You two have got to get used to the fact that there are lots of people out there interested in the multiage concept. Just pretend that you are talking to fifteen or twenty people, rather than 150 plus."

"Plus?"

"Oh, we're still getting out-of-state registrations," she admitted blithely. "We'll cut it off at 200."

Fortunately, the numbers had not increased significantly. Unfortunately, our nervousness had. Where were all these people coming from? We began to find out. We got a call from Diane Olds, a teacher in Nevada, "Can a group of us meet with you at the conference? We're involved in multiage, and we'd love to bounce ideas back and forth." Jane Dopheide, a colleague from a course we were taking spoke to us in class. "I'm excited about your presentation! My district has been planning our multiage program and I'm anxious to hear about the way you do it." Our friend Corda Ladd, consulting resource teacher in our school, was a person who got around: "Oh, yes! Everywhere I go people are talking multiage. It's definitely the new direction in education. Wake up, you guys!"

We gave ourselves a shake and woke up. We acknowledged that maybe we had isolated ourselves a bit. We had been so wrapped up in refining our own program, planning our book, and teaching our kids that we had not looked outward to see the varying directions that multiage education was taking. We discussed this problem as we got together to plan our presentation.

"So here we are with 150 people coming to hear us talk, and probably most of them know more about multiage education than we do!" I agonized.

"We can only tell them what we are doing now. We've never claimed to be experts," Jane reassured me. "We're still trying to figure it out ourselves!"

"Well, we'll just have to tell people that," I suggested. "I know, let's do this presentation as a play. We'll sit and talk together about our program. About how we are changing all the time, discovering new things to try, and always thinking about how we can improve."

"Good idea! If we can't talk with our audience, at least we can talk to each other," Jane commented. "Since we want to show slides of our class, we can pretend that we're sorting through them to decide which ones to use."

"And in the process, we will be telling them about what we do! It sounds great!" I raved.

That was then. The morning of the conference, it didn't sound so good. What if we got up on stage and couldn't think of what to say? What if the audience didn't understand that we were doing a play? What if they didn't laugh at our jokes? What if all our ideas were old hat?

It is almost hard to remember the jitters and stage fright now. The audience *was* receptive to our ideas and polite about our jokes. We could feel that they were with us after our second line. They clapped warmly for us at the end and kept us on stage long afterwards answering their questions. Still heady with success, we met with the Nevada teachers. Ideas flew as we exchanged information and shared perspectives. What a wealth of expertise we were discovering all of a sudden! "Won't you write a section for our book on metacognition in a multiage classroom, Claudia? And you, Wanda, could you tell about the specialist's role? Tamara, could you do curriculum development? Diane, what will you do? The qualities necessary for being a multiage teacher? Sounds great!"

The Re-Imagining Schools conference was an eye-opener for us. It was the catalyst that revitalized our mental wheels and got them spinning again. Through our contacts there we became aware of the overwhelming interest in multiage education. We also began to reflect on the differences and commonalities that exist in multiage philosophies. In the weeks to follow we earnestly began designing our book about multiage grouping. Almost magically, it seemed, long-lost friends and acquaintances with unique perspectives on multiage education began popping into our lives almost everywhere we went. We discovered multiage connections at weddings, parties, and courses. We realized that input from these people would enrich our story. We invited them to write for us.

These folks kind of fell into our laps. But when we started *looking* for examples of multiage education, we were amazed at what we found. Multiage education is everywhere in this country. It is in rural Maine. It is in the inner cities of Reno, Nevada, and Louisville, Kentucky. It is in private schools for the behaviorally dysfunctional and in schools for the advantaged. It is in preschools, elementary schools, and middle schools. People all over are talking about it and writing about it. Parents, administrators, academians, and special educators are championing the multiage cause. We call this section of our book *Ripples* to indicate the widening circles of multiage practices. This first chapter in the section is an amalgamation of insights from a diverse group of practitioners who are developing aspects of their multiage programs. Following this chapter are chapters written by a variety of multiage educators from across the United States. We hope that the stories told in this section will convince our readers that multiage education is for everyone.

Beginnings

Jane and I developed our multiage program to address inadequacies we perceived in standard graded environments. We saw some needs, we considered them for a time, and then we joined together to leap in feet first to do what we could to make changes. People embrace multiage teaching for different reasons and in different ways. But multiage educators have some attributes in common.

··◆··◆··◆··◆···

Diane Olds is a primary multiage teacher at the Agnes Risley School near Reno, Nevada. She explores the qualities of "typical" multiage educators by reflecting on her own growth as she developed a multiage program with her peers.

> *WANTED: Elementary teacher willing to teach three grade levels in one classroom. Requirements: Must be organized, willing to take risks, flexible, knowledgeable in the area of child development, committed to the teaching profession, cognizant of the need for continual professional growth, able to organize and integrate curriculum, dissatisfied with traditional, bureaucratic grouping of students.*

A classified ad for multiage teachers might look like this one. Why would anyone take on such a challenge?

Successful multigrade teachers begin with a fundamental belief that a traditional school model does not meet the needs of children. Even before we encountered multiage group classrooms, we moved away from a textbook/cookbook curriculum, grouped children in new ways, and began to look for an educational paradigm that matched our instinct that the mandated curriculum did not address students' developmental levels. Multiage teachers are reflective, metacognitive self-inquirers who enjoy puzzling through what we do not yet fully understand. We are comfortable saying, "We don't have the answer to that right now." This attitude is reflected in our classrooms, as we say to students, "There are not always right answers to questions." We constantly ask ourselves, "Why?" and "Why not?" We seek out our peers to reflect aloud, to find sounding boards, to seek counsel, and to engage in genuine dialogue. As we search for more answers, we spend much time discussing children, education, and personal philosophy. We would rather be challenged and teetering on the brink of an exciting venture than be safe and bored. We confidently approach our newly configured classrooms, even though success may be unsure.

Multiage teachers are curriculum and child development specialists. We recognize the importance of both elements to the educational paradigm and are able to apply our knowledge about teaching and development in designing effective instructional practices. We are able to look beyond the boundaries and restrictions of our own grade levels. As we make curricular decisions for our own multiage programs, we have a clear vision of where students have come from and where they are headed. We integrate and weave subjects together within a three-year cycle to build a model of the contemporary integrated curriculum. We have analyzed the total spectrum of the elementary school curriculum, and we have a vision of how different subject areas can be interconnected. While we accept responsibility for teaching certain topics, we understand that they can and should be rearranged for optimal learning connections.

Multiage teachers see their children as symbiotic members of a learning community, and we teach them to be helpmates who give and receive assistance based on individual strengths and needs. We value our students as independent problem-solvers who are able and expected to function without constant teacher intervention and direction. We see ourselves as facilitators rather than knowledge dispensers. Visiting teachers often express astonishment at the on-task behavior of individual students and groups while the teacher works with a small group in a corner. This classroom behavior is a reflection of the teachers' beliefs that children can eagerly direct their own learning. Multiage teachers are unafraid to give up power to reach our more important goal of creating self-directed lifelong lovers of learning.

Multiage teachers apply appropriate instructional practices. We choose to do it in a multigrade setting because we recognize that children do not progress in tidy one-year linear growth patterns. We would eagerly answer the ad for a multiage teacher!

◆··◆··◆··◆

A need to question the status quo seems to characterize multiage educators. Jane Dopheide teaches in a primary school in Winterport, Maine. She describes how the questions of the faculty in her school resulted in the creation of a multiage program.

The multiage classrooms in our school were established through the hard work of group process and change. Our school of 348 children is situated in a rural community of 3,200 people on the Penobscot river near Bangor, Maine. The people of our community work on the land, in the woods, and in professions within the greater Bangor area. We are more conservative than liberal, with strong feelings for our town and our schools. For years, teachers had operated comfortably behind closed doors, coming together occasionally to eat, and to share brief anecdotes, but not to communicate about the day-to-day business of learning.

In 1987, concerns about readiness, retention, and the concept of developmental learning led us to move toward educational change.

Many of the teachers in our school became involved in self-study, workshops, visits to transitional programs, and ongoing staff discussions. An Early Childhood Grant in 1988 enabled us to establish a pre-first classroom for children who were not ready for the traditional expectations of first grade. This program proved to be a healthier, more productive alternative to retention. More importantly, it stimulated discussion between teachers, administrators, and parents about ways to improve the entire primary grade program for all children.

The next step that emerged in the change process was an evaluation and subsequent revision of our K-2 report card. Most of the staff felt the existing card did not reflect children's developmental learning processes. With the aid of report card examples from other districts, we created a progress report through a consensus process that incorporated our concerns about developmental education. When the administration approved the card, it was a major victory that empowered us as professionals and established within our staff a higher level of trust.

Our new reporting system kept alive discussions about ways to improve the entire K-2 program for all children, and it led us to multiage learning/teaching. We talked about sharing children's progress in learning and about the wide range of developmental levels found within our classrooms. With our principal as a major player, we broke down the barriers created by grade levels and moved away from the pre-first concept. Through more self-study, visitations, and summer workshops, we collected additional information on multiage learning and teaching.

In the weekly meetings of the next school year some of us shared the knowledge and enthusiasm we had acquired in the summer workshops. Others expressed strong skepticism about multiage concepts. These meeting were tense, unlike our meetings on report cards and on the pre-first program. Some teachers sat apart from the group, while others stopped coming to the meetings. Our communication broke down. The multiage classroom discussions challenged long-held attitudes and beliefs about the education of children. Proponents and opponents raised many questions about multiage classrooms. Should five-year-olds be included? Could we risk overwhelming them in their first year of school? Why were we discarding the pre-first program? Would children currently served by the pre-first be absorbed into the multiage classrooms? If so, would this make the multiage classrooms unbalanced? Who had the experience to teach in the multiage classrooms? Would seven-year-olds be sufficiently challenged in the presence of so many younger children? Would teachers or parents choose the students to be placed in the multiage classrooms? Would the classrooms be heterogeneous?

For three months all of the questions were discussed by groups of teachers and our principal. In spite of misgivings by some, we decided to invite community reaction to the multiage concept. The very positive responses we received from parents who attended our first informational meeting led to the formation of an advisory committee. This group of parents, teachers, our principal, and a school board member continued the exploration. Committee members visited multiage classrooms in other schools, developed a multiage brochure for parents, and generated feedback and support for the process. After two presentations to our school board, we received approval to pilot two multiage classrooms for three years.

Two additional informational meetings were held in the spring. Parents were asked to make a choice for their children. At one of these informational meetings teachers and parents from a nearby district talked about their three years of experience with a multiage program, and they answered questions raised by our parents. The meetings also afforded us opportunities to describe the program we planned to provide in our school.

After a year of working in a multiage program, questions and concerns are still under discussion. Hopefully, the dialogue between teachers, administrators, and parents will continue. For teachers, the most important question ahead of us is the toughest one. How do we continue to work together within our imperfect system to open the doors of our classrooms wider? To answer this question we must learn to share our successes and our failures along with our doubts and discoveries. Through this kind of inquiry we will create a community of learners of all ages in which we can effectively continue our quest for an educational system that fits children and their families.

We are impressed with Winterport's comprehensive process for implementing their multiage program. It is so different from our more gut-level, "just do it" approach. Acting as a committee of two, we were able to get our multiage classes up and going in a matter of months. However, we see definite advantages in the way Winterport involved all the staff in exploring and designing their new program. We suspect that Winterport's program will expand naturally, because everyone participated in the ground floor discussions and gained the same knowledge base. To counteract confusion, fear, and isolation, the Winterport staff has set a precedent for dealing with issues and questions through healthy dialogue. However, change is never easy. Even when elaborate groundwork has been done and a successful program has been established, that program does not just naturally become self-sustaining.

◆·◆··◆·◆

Carol Carriuolo's concern for the education of her child resulted in the creation of a multiage program called MILE (Multiage Integrated Learning Environment) in her Unity, Maine, district. Carol was the guiding force in the extensive process of creating MILE, which also resulted in a new career for herself as a teacher advisor and consultant. Carol is well aware of the complexities of the change process.

My daughter was just four years old when my questions about schooling began. I was experiencing that curious mixture of joy and pain that comes when parents watch their child develop autonomy and begin meaningful relationships outside of the family. One day soon, I knew, she would be leaving home to participate in what is expected of all children—SCHOOL! Or would she? Living in a rural area limited educational alternatives to a few private schools. The potential isolation of an only child did not make home schooling an appealing choice. I valued the public school system as a part of community life, but I had so many questions. "Why is it that our young children are passively fed content? Why is it that as a parent I have no choice about the environment or the person my child is about to spend over 1,000 hours with each year? Why is it that what is known and well-documented about how young children grow and develop has little influence on curriculum? How is this new surge of pressure to reform schools and compete academically going to affect my child?" I wanted answers to my questions before even considering registering her for kindergarten.

Feelings of panic and protection moved me to find a clear direction and take action. I met with the superintendent of schools in my district. He listened to my questions and my recommendations. We discovered that we were both committed to looking at how to meet the needs of the district's primary-age children. A committee of diverse individuals including teachers, parents, and administrators was formed. The next year and a half we devoted to research, discussion, observation, argument, grant writing, and public debate.

What did we discover? In spite of our differences in approach, values, and experience we agreed that the single-graded content-oriented curriculum was not the only structure for primary education. What emerged was the idea that by removing grade-level boundaries, we might create a model in which children of various ages could work together in a nurturing atmosphere. Such a model would honor differences in learning style and time tables, while simultaneously recognizing common goals for cognitive, physical, social, and emotional growth. These classrooms would strive to reflect current knowledge about child development and appropriate classroom practices.

Three years of being engrossed in creating MILE and consulting with other districts interested in multiage programs led me to the realization that what was really happening was all about the process of making fundamental change. People were beginning to shift their perceptions about schooling and about what could be possible in this rural community. We have created a program, and in doing so, we have catapulted ourselves and others into the process of change, which includes disequilibrium. For some, this state of flux is unwelcome. Just as the development of children naturally includes periods of disequilibrium and does not proceed in a straight line, neither does successful change and the people affected. Fortunately, the decentralized approach to the development of MILE provided a forum where collaboration and collective vision-making are taken seriously. This process continues to be extremely hard work.

Offering a different educational program has created an edge. MILE supporters are forced to act politically, forced to be clear with their language, forced to justify their choice. Although this edge is sometimes painful, it serves an important purpose. We cannot remain complacent. We must continue to ask hard questions of ourselves and of the people within the system to whom we entrust our children. We must demand the best for our children and for our world and act assertively to see that these demands are addressed. This edge is not just about creating the MILE program. I am clear about that. This edge is about change.

I see teachers and parents successfully creating an environment and community of support for themselves as they carve away at the culture's notion of "school." These people are learners and risk-takers, willing to ask hard questions and proceed without hard answers. They demand active administrative support and involvement. They are able to steel themselves to criticism and apathy by their colleagues and friends. They are working at becoming articulate spokespeople for their ideas. They have opened the doors and welcomed wide participation. But most of all, they acknowledge that their process brings up feelings of disequilibrium. They accept their disequilibrium and trust that periods of unease must occur before they can attain a more mature stage of equilibrium. I am proud to be associated with these people, and to have had a hand in opening this door to successful change.

◆··◆··◆··◆

Keeping It Going

As the previous two writings illustrate, beginnings are exciting, but they can also be rough going. We wondered how many multiage programs withstand the test of time. Would anyone have the energy to maintain a multiage program after expending the necessary effort to get one going? Again, the experiences of two of our educator friends gave us insight and hope. Both are teachers in ongoing and long-lasting multiage programs.

◆··◆··◆··◆

Betsy Siebert teaches in a multiage preschool that has been in operation for twenty-five years. Her description of the school shows us why it has continued to be successful for so many years.

The Barn Coop Nursery School in Concord, Massachusetts, is a non-profit, parent-run preschool committed to mixed age grouping. It began twenty-five years ago when a group of parents decided to start a nursery school that would foster an extended family atmosphere. In this setting adults and children would know and care about each other. These parents wanted to create a learning environment that would reflect the way children learn at home. The environment was designed to encourage maximum involvement of the children and offer various opportunities for self-initiated creative play. The school was based on the idea that a child should be actively involved in making decisions and free to follow his or her own curiosity. The membership would consist of twenty-one three-, four-, and five-year-olds mixed together with three teachers and one parent helper each day. They decided to use multiage grouping because it best resembled family grouping. Also, most children in multiage groupings stay together for two to three years, thus making it possible to form long-lasting, close relationships among children, parents, and teachers.

As a cooperative, the Barn also provides parents with a wonderful chance for self-enrichment. All parents, regardless of their experience in interacting with children, have something of value to bring to the classroom. Children benefit as much from exposure to diverse personalities and lifestyles as they do from a variety of projects and materials. The parent members hire the director, aid in hiring the teachers, help set the educational goals, and assist in the classroom.

At the Barn, the children provide each other with a rich environment not available in a group restricted to a single age. Children vary widely in their rates of development, and in a mixed-age group they can choose their playmates according to their own feelings and personal development on any given day. Children learn through imitation, observation, and exploration. Mixed age grouping provides the children with opportunities to lead, follow, nurture, take risks, and practice skills.

One day after a storm we found many large tree limbs lying in our playground. Willy, one of the older, capable five-year-olds, came up with an idea. He wanted to build a tree fort using all the branches. He asked one of the teachers for a saw, a hammer, and some nails. He attempted to cut one of the smaller branches off a limb with the saw, but he found it was too difficult to do alone. Brian, one of the younger, less capable children, offered to help hold the tree branch steady. Soon it became clear that they needed more helpers. At first, the other boys and girls were not willing to help. Brian suggested to Willy that he give everyone a turn to cut off a branch, if they would help hold the tree limb steady. Indeed, the other children, younger and older, were willing to help if they got to have a turn. Willy, who directed the group, let everyone have a turn and then managed to extend the play even further. Some of the children followed him with their branches, hammers, and nails to build their own tree fort!

In this situation Willy was able to experience being a leader, a teacher, and a cooperative playmate. Brian felt welcomed and valued, and Willy felt competent and successful. The other children were inspired to work together, take turns, and offer assistance to those less capable. For some children it was the first time they had ever attempted to cut with a saw.

The presence of older children can sometimes create pressure on the younger children. This pressure may cause cognitive conflict and anxiety. However, with the proper guidance and support, this pressure stimulates growth. In one example, Christen, a younger three-year-old, was asked to write her name on her completed art project. She immediately responded, "But I can't write my name!" Ricky, a four-year-old who was working near her at the same table, simply said, "Oh, I can write it for you!" The younger children appreciate being cared for by the older ones and quickly reveal their own skills in a desire to be as able as their elders.

In a multiage preschool setting these are two examples of how children are valued for their talents and the contributions they can make to the whole group. They develop an awareness of their own needs and how to meet them. They are helped to learn by children both older and younger than themselves. Most importantly, they become more sensitive to the needs and feelings of others. At the Barn, we not only believe that multiage grouping works, we feel strongly that it is the most natural atmosphere in which to promote children's growth.

◆ ◆ ◆ ◆

Another long-term veteran of multiage, Dave Carman, taught at the Sidwell Friends School in Washington, DC, which has been offering a multiage option to its fifth and sixth graders for eleven years. In his writing Dave explores the reasons why multiage works for these older students. Dave maintains that even the time spent away from school in the summer contributes significantly to the growth of students in a multiage class.

The first days of school in September were filled with anticipation. My homeroom consisted of ten to twelve returning sixth graders and the same number of new fifth graders. I always knew the sixth graders well because almost all of them had been in my homeroom as fifth graders the year before. These fifth graders were new. They looked around my open classroom with wonder and expectation. Years before, the faculty and administration at Sidwell Friends School, in Northwest Washington, DC, had decided to offer a range of instruction styles for students in the Middle School, grades five through eight. One option for fifth- and sixth-grade students was a multiage classroom. This classroom would have a cozy reading area, lots of tables, a meeting area, individual desks in little nooks and crannies, and lots of different groups all working at different rates in texts chosen to meet those students' needs. It would be taught by a dynamic, perhaps a little whimsical, teacher, who adjusted the work to meet individual needs and didn't give grades.

That was my room. Since there was no other room exactly like it, the fifth graders began the year in September with some sense of awe. They could sense the warmth and positive spirit that the returning sixth graders brought back to the room each fall. They could feel the stimulation in the displays of creative writing and books. They could overhear stories about last year.

The returning sixth graders were feeling very different emotions. First, they knew what to expect. This room was familiar. I was a known quantity. And, perhaps most important of all, they knew what I wanted from each of them this year. During the year, I always talk individually with the students about their strengths and weaknesses, so at the end of the fifth-grade year, students left for summer vacation with a reasonably clear sense of what they needed to improve. And it often seemed that over the summer those goals simmered in their souls. When the lid came off in September, the flavor was more robust than in June. Students were able to perform in ways that had seemed out of reach last June.

One area of summer skill growth that always stood out, in part because I had numerical data to pinpoint the growth, was spelling skills. We always administered the Lincoln Spelling Test at the beginning and end of each year, so I had each returning student's score from the previous late May. About 70 percent of the returning group gained points.

This was not the only area where students returned from the summer "vacation" with skills they had not shown the previous June. Organization skills was another. Many students who had struggled to complete assignments on time seemed noticeably better at this task as sixth graders. A third area that improved involved writing in complete sentences, a task that was an impossible hurdle for a few fifth graders. As in the other areas, they seemed miraculously able to do this when they returned as sixth graders, even though they had had no formal instruction or practice over the summer.

There is no doubt that students grow and mature over the summer. In most cases, a break from school provides a chance to recharge batteries. People often integrate new skills and develop new resolve when they are given time to step back from a difficult situation. It is common for students to enter a new year with the September equivalent of New Year's resolutions. These explanations for summer growth are true for all kinds of classrooms, yet I believe there is no evidence for summer growth as pronounced as I experienced between fifth- and sixth-grade years in a multiage classroom.

The critical feature of a multiage classroom is that students are returning to the same teacher. I believe the growth I observed was so noticeable because students were familiar with the kinds of tasks they were going to have to improve at, and because they identified with the familiar teacher who would notice and approve the changes. I believe that identification with the adult teacher was an especially powerful motivation for summer growth. This notion was occasionally confirmed in an offhand way when students would seek out my reaction to their new abilities. It was clear they knew I'd be proud of them and they wanted me to know they were proud of themselves.

Having students for two years was helpful from my point of view. It allowed me to approach many critical developmental tasks with a two-year perspective. If fraction division, spelling rules, prepositional phrases, writing in complete sentences, etc., were proving difficult, I could break these tasks down and encourage students to bite off only a part of it now, knowing we had all next year to finish up with it. Often students learned better when they were aware that the pressure was off.

The multiage group also facilitated the adjustment new students had to make. Their sense of wonder, of not being "sure," was quickly replaced by commitment to the new environment and teacher. Even in the first week of school, I could sense them relaxing. And I knew that the older students were answering their questions, helping them out, teaching them the ropes, and subtly conveying the message that the classroom "worked." Just by being there, they encouraged the new students to be swept up in the excitement of the multiage classroom.

◆··◆··◆··◆

Creating Environments for Learning

Dave's point is well-made. The pressure *is* off students in multiage classes. Multiage teachers all agree that time is on our side. Teaching and learning in multiage settings takes on a depth that is not possible in single-grade classes. Still, multiage teachers are often asked, "How do you cover the curriculum? How do you decide what to teach and when to teach it?"

◆··◆··◆··◆

Tamara Baren, who teaches in a suburb of Reno, Nevada, explores some curricular issues.

The greatest challenge a multiage teacher faces is neither meshing a wide spectrum of students, nor planting the seeds of community. Instead, it lies in developing an approach to the curriculum that satisfies state and local demands, while supporting the students' and teachers' ongoing learning partnership. The question of management of the three-year curriculum cycle in multiage classrooms draws our attention to the underlying vision that guides curriculum choices: educating children.

Curriculum choices in multiage classrooms spring from the conviction that learning is a fluid process, in which the essential factors of rehearsal, approximation, and interpretation find honor. Multiage learning structures draw from the knowledge that children grow loosely through certain patterns or stages of social, emotional, and cognitive development. Progress is not necessarily uniform or matched to age or grade levels. The goals of multiage curriculum planning must be to foster an active learning relationship and to accommodate the developmental diversity inherent in a multiage community.

Multiage teachers manipulate curriculum to restructure traditional linear sequencing, presentation, and skill practice into a meaningful, contextually rich theme study. Language plays a central role in learning here. Writing, speaking, observing, and dialogue serve to expand and define students' perceptions. Process-based formats in the language arts, such as Writers' and Readers' Workshops, allow teachers to model whole group strategies and work with individuals or small flexible groups. A skeleton of small group work in the specific areas of math and word study supports whole group theme-centered collaborations.

Successful management of the complex three-year curriculum relies on two factors. They are the manipulation of curriculum requirements into an integrated cycle of subjects, and the selection of activities that consolidate multiple curriculum needs. To achieve a comprehensive curriculum, teachers need an overview of the mastery levels of the three-year cycle and the components at each grade level. Teachers need a knowledge of the repeated strands within subject areas. Teachers must make a careful examination of the kinds of knowledge required in particular topic areas.

Many teachers find that assembling a visual map of the theme helps to organize and prioritize the possibilities. Through the mapping process natural relationships between subject areas appear, allowing the teacher to begin consolidating and interweaving goals toward the theme. Once the major elements of the unit are in place, planning focuses on selecting activities and experiences that build higher level thinking and encourage students to practice cognitive strategies. Each activity must be multi-purposed in order to meet curriculum demands. Higher level cognitive exercises are balanced with concrete expressions such as art, cooking, and dramatic performance. Complex activities tackled in cooperative groups, informal groups, and cross-age partnerships accommodate the naturally wide range of strengths and abilities inherent in multiage structures. Not every unit of study will reflect involvement in all subjects equally. Therefore, maintaining a three-year overview of goals and topics becomes crucial in everyday decision making and planning.

A theme of exploration, for example, may be the umbrella for many related activities in an intermediate classroom. Students can study the process of mapping and geography, European explorers and the dynamics of the times in which they lived, and the explorers' impact on indigenous peoples. Simulations could allow whole group work in math areas of measurement, computation, and logic as students outfit their ships and crews for journeys. Students might practice research techniques, write journals and pop-up books about the explorers, and engage in value discussions on the issues of the times. They would learn study skills and techniques in content area reading and writing, and, later in the unit, would learn all about design, scale, and portrait painting in the process of creating a mural to share their learning. Interwoven into the theme of exploration might be the study of the open ocean, water salinity and currents, global climate, and marine life.

The process and products of thematic study over a three-year period reflect a global approach toward curriculum organization. They promote a revisioning of what classroom work might look like outside the realm of traditional teacher-directed instruction. Teachers' roles shift toward guiding student learning processes, suggesting study possibilities, providing the tools of investigation, and developing in students a meta-cognitive awareness of their own learning progress and potential.

Through all multiage study work runs a common thread of partnership in learning. Students' experiences, ideas, and questions form an important component of unit development. Curriculum management for multiage classes means active incorporation of student interests and direction, and a democratic format in classroom dynamics. Multiage teachers seek to create learning contexts for their students where the need for literacy and refined skills in thinking, problem solving, and inquiry make satisfying sense.

As Tamara suggests, a more global curriculum is the result of the luxury of time that multiage settings offer. But we all know that there is more to teaching than curriculum.

◆··◆··◆··◆

Another of our Nevada associates, Claudia Rossi, finds that a multiage environment is an ideal place to teach children *how* to learn.

Learning evolves from the social interaction of an expert and a novice. Success of a multiage classroom is rooted in a structure that promotes the perception that we are all learners, regardless of age. The teacher is seen as part of the community of learners and acts as facilitator within the structure. The range of age and experience, coupled with the relationship of the group over an extended time frame, are essential components of metacognitive development. We work from a child's knowledge base to help him or her make meaning. A wide range of levels in the classroom provides children with an exposure to many people who already understand a concept or who have had an experience that will help a child learn. The teacher and the children become the scaffolding support needed for learners to reach independent levels of performance. For children to feel secure enough to question and work with others in developing strategies for learning, they must have a great deal of trust. Multiage classrooms provide the time element needed for students to get to know the teacher and classmates. Given this time, they feel free enough to expose their thoughts and ask questions. This structure impacts the learners' personal understanding of how both the individual and the group works to acquire knowledge. Teachers work within the multiage classrooms providing experiences for children to bring their knowledge from the tacit to the overt by helping develop knowledge about their own thinking.

In practice this means that we are asking students to become aware of what they know and be able to identify it, express it, and analyze it. Through teacher and peer modeling, students internalize the kinds of questions that give them the language of thought. This essential part of the multiage model permeates everything in the classroom, all day long, every day, at all grade levels. In both social and curricular areas, students are asked: What do you know? What do you want to know? Where can you get information? What went well? Why? Where were there problems? What can you do about it? Where can you go from here? As these types of open-ended questions are asked, dialogue ensues between student and teacher or student and student. Eventually, the students ask these questions themselves. This aids in their understanding of how they need to get information for personal understanding.

As we are helping children develop knowledge about social situations, the everyday exercise of recess can provide an arena for concept building. The teacher might dialogue with students with questions such as the following: What is recess for? What are some of the activities that you might do during this time? How do you get someone to play with you? How can you handle differing opinions in your play group? How can the group decide on how to play before you start? What do you do when someone wants to join your game? Following the activity, the teacher again provides questioning strategies by posing statements like these: What went well at recess? Why did it go so well? Was there a problem? Why do you think it happened? What do you think would make it a better situation next time? This type of question, modeled and practiced over time, helps students to assess what it is they need to do to have fun in a social situation. Our students begin to realize that adults do not solve all the problems; they begin to exert personal control over social interactions. Students begin to build a reservoir of strategies that enable them to function effectively with a group.

Throughout various curricular activities, our students must be taught strategies that enable them to take their learning beyond present knowledge. In this process, it is essential that teachers be aware of the levels of the student knowledge in order to provide appropriate materials and experiences for them. During a class unit of study about space, questions such as "What do you know about the solar system?"; "What do you want to know?"; and "How can you find information to answer your questions?" would give the teacher information about what concepts about the topic the class understands, or what misconceptions need to be clarified. As students become familiar with this line of questioning and reflection, they are able to address what they know about a topic and bring forth that prior knowledge in support of new information. When students are asked what they want to learn, they give focus to the subject at hand. A feeling of control and ownership of information brings personal meaning to the task. If our students are to grow to be independent, life-long learners, we need to teach strategies that enable them to know where and how to gain information. By asking students how they might find information, the teacher opens the subject to a wealth of answers that provide information about resources beyond the teacher. A final question might be "What did you learn?" As we ask our students to reflect upon what has been learned, they begin to develop knowledge about what they have to do in order to develop personal understandings.

Through teaching metacognitive strategies, we show students how to build upon what they know and how to tackle what they don't know. We strive for an awareness in our students that causes them to say, "Yes, I can!" Indeed, it is our responsibility as teachers to help students see the importance of life-long learning and know how to acquire knowledge.

◆ ◆ ◆ ◆

Supporting Roles

We believe that people of all ages can learn well in multiage environments. We see multiage groups all around us. A group of women gets together for a monthly writing group; the women range in age from thirty-two to fifty years. The 10:00 A.M. class at a nearby stable contains four students: two six-year-olds, a ten-year-old, and a twenty-eight-year-old circle the ring on their mounts, receiving instruction from the teacher in the center. At the fitness center in town, classes in yoga, aerobics, and dance are multiaged. Choruses, theater groups, art classes, soccer leagues—the list could go on and on—are multiaged as a matter of course. We can learn different things from people of different ages.

◆ ◆ ◆ ◆

Our good friend, Corda Ladd, whose background in special education makes her especially cognizant of how to meet children's needs, comments in bewilderment, "Isn't it strange that the only place in society where we ask people to work in their own age group is in schools?" Corda knows that multiage groups can work for children of all abilities.

The idea of educating children with differing ages is not new to the special educator. Educating children with disabilities in a regular multiage setting *is* new. Many educators and parents are coming to believe children with disabilities will reach their full potential and become self-reliant only if they receive their education in the mainstream. In this context students have access to the same social and educational opportunities as their non-handicapped peers. Teachers are leaving the safe and old way of segregated settings for an exciting and inclusive way of educating children with disabilities. In the 1990s the model of a consulting resource teacher emerged. The goal of this model is cooperative, interdependent programming in which several adults with differing and complimentary skills come together in the interest of a student to problem solve short-term and long-term objectives for him or her. In this way the needs of the child are met in the child's world, rather than in a separate room off to the side.

The relationship of the multiage teacher and the resource teacher is the platform on which the work with the children is built. Their relationship must be created and continuously nurtured. In order to meet the child's needs, teachers who are collaborating must let go of their own territorial, ownership, and power needs. This process deserves much attention if a resource teacher intends to be successful working in the multiage classroom, rather than in isolation.

There is not just one way for educators to collaborate; instead there are a range of possibilities. The way the multiage teacher and the special teacher decide to work together depends on previous role definitions, relationships, flexibility, and scheduling, as well as the strengths and weaknesses of the identified student. The choices are to take the identified child out of the classroom or to work within the classroom. The possibilities for working in the classroom include one-on-one tutoring, small group instruction, and team teaching to co-create ways to meet the students' needs.

Working with children of differing abilities, ages, and stages is possible if the focus is on strategies rather than individual skills. Strategies that successful learners use are often not visible to learners who struggle. The teacher's job is to make these strategies visible. The use of metacognition plays a starring role here. Small group processing at any time in the lesson allows all the learners to see how a peer solves a problem, figures out a word, or makes meaning out of confusion.

One effective way to move toward inclusive education is to facilitate a literature study group within the classroom. In a literature group the specialist works with a heterogeneous group as the members read and study a piece of children's literature. The group consists of the student with special needs and approximately six other students, who have all self-selected this book. In this setting the student with a disability can learn from strong peer models. The specialist makes sure that appropriate skills are being presented in context and in an authentic setting. The classroom teacher's load is lightened by the presence of another educator in the classroom.

Setting the tone of the ways students will work together is the responsibility of all the teachers. Working with children of multi-ages and multi-stages must be accomplished in an atmosphere of high expectations. Teachers must ask for each person's best work, deepest learning, and constant improvement on his or her own level.

By supporting, championing, and facilitating learning in a multiage setting, teachers can help all students. The challenges are finding joint planning time, scheduling, problem solving, and nurturing working relationships. The successes for educators who work together are peer support, a sharing of ideas and strategies, a synergy that is created by people working together towards a common goal, student academic gains, and happier students.

◆ ◆ ◆ ◆

As educators widen their perspectives they see that varying abilities and wide ranges of development can be accommodated in multiage groups. As classroom teachers are embracing the multiage system, they are helping other special teachers to see how multiage groups can work successfully for them, too. Wanda Nomura writes about the role of specialists in multiage settings.

Traditionally, specialists play an important role as a significant support system for the regular classroom teacher. These instructors assist in the enrichment and/or the remediation of the students through activities in their areas of expertise. The classroom teacher also relies upon the specialist to gain more in-depth knowledge about a specific curriculum area. Typically, specialists include teachers of music, physical education, computer science, library science, gifted and talented, and remedial and special education.

Oftentimes, the linear nature of the specialists' jobs results in a specialized focus in curriculum study. Time constraints restrict their view of the global nature of the classroom community. With only a limited amount of student contact, the inclination is to concentrate more fully on the specific subject area rather than view the curriculum as integrated and continuous. As in the fable of the blind men and the elephant, these instructors glimpse only a small portion of the students' learning environment, culminating in a curriculum of narrow or isolated focus, not in keeping with the students' whole learning progression.

The role of the specialist as a support system continues in today's multiage class. However, the composition of a class containing three grade levels for a three-year span encourages the reevaluation of the structure of the specialist's program. The person who envisions and embraces the philosophy of the multiage program will appreciate the changes brought about in a curriculum where children learn in an integrated manner. The range of concepts and activities that can be employed with the students in this learning process is vast; they are, however, dependent upon the willingness of the specialist to remodel existing programs. The extent of the modifications made is dependent upon the pre-multiage teaching style of the specialist. In one Nevada school, a recently-hired physical education teacher found little difficulty in gauging the type of activities to accommodate the range of abilities within the multiage class. The children were not only cooperative, but were also cognizant of the diverse developmental stages displayed by their classmates. Students accepted and adjusted to the ability levels present in group situations. When applicable, the instructor attempted to reflect the classroom learning theme by using physical education as the vehicle to extend curricular knowledge. On the other hand, anxious specialists voiced negative thoughts about the amount of time, energy, and effort to be expended upon the reorganization of their established programs. Fortunately, not everyone viewed reconstruction as a negative force. One veteran music teacher expressed apprehension in being able to meet the needs of such a vast range of development and voice abilities of three different age groups. She not only discovered harmonic blending with the wider range of voices, but challenged herself to incorporate curriculum themes into her lesson plans to support and enhance the units of study of the regular class. Specialists who share the vision of global learning make it possible to extend the multiage concept to other curriculum areas.

Restructuring special education programs has lately become an area of interest. Conventional special education programs are "pull-out"—exclusive—programs where students leave their classrooms to attend an individual or a small group setting in a separate environment. With the advocacy of "push-in"—inclusive—programs, special education students are now being included in the multiage setting. Students are grouped to learn skills and strategies that mirror the theme and skills being taught to the whole class. It allows the children who need continuity throughout their daily regimen to concentrate and focus upon learning strategies with their fellow students while experiencing less stigma and isolation from their peers. Classroom teachers feel the inclusive program supports continuity of learning, is less disruptive and more focused, and contributes to the growth of a positive self-image for the student with special needs.

Open dialogue between the regular classroom teacher and the specialist is a necessary component to maximize learning. Ideas and opinions must be tossed about or refined in an accepting environment where all who are involved feel safe in expressing their thoughts. Many informal "chat" sessions are on-going and maintain a sense of commitment to each student's success. All team members need to know that mutual respect permeates the learning environment surrounding the student. The feeling of being an empowered member of a team in which all share a similar vision will heighten the appeal for successful and cooperative alliances. It works for the adults just as it does for the students.

◆··◆··◆··◆

Recently, we were asked to facilitate a monthly multiage support group. The group, to be known as a reflective practice group, was sponsored by the Western Maine Partnership out of the University of Maine at Farmington. Its director, Margaret Arbuckle, pressed us for organizational details. "What will you call your group?" she asked.

"Multiage Mania!" we responded, laughing. Unfortunately, the name stuck. But when the group began to meet, we were overwhelmed at the monthly response. Teachers, administrators, and parents, some new to multiage and some veterans, were coming from all over central Maine to learn more about multiage education. We focused our sessions around the group members' questions. There were many: How do we get started? How do we educate the public? How do we meet the needs of all those different levels? What ages work best together? How can we help special teachers adjust to multiage? What does a typical day in a multiage classroom look like? How will we evaluate the students? Again, we were surprised by the intensity of interest in the multiage concept. It is apparent that people out there want to know about multiage! We continue to find that there is never a shortage of questions. We hope that this chapter has addressed some of the issues and concerns that are on people's minds. The *Ripples* section of this book continues with four more chapters written by educators coming from a variety of settings across the country. The mulitage circle is widening.

Multiage
A Parent's View

Katy Alioto

If I ask myself as a parent what I most want for my children—my heart-felt desires—my answers are decidedly qualitative rather than quantitative. I hope that my children will feel fulfilled and content without being narrowly self-satisfied, that they will give and receive others' respect, that they will be critical thinkers, that they will contribute constructively to their society, and that they will face adversity with courage, intelligence, and patience. My children have been schooled in a multiage environment. This multiage vehicle has helped my children move toward successful maturation.

Multiage groupings include two characteristics not duplicated by single-grade classes. These characteristics are significant student differences and continuity of learning over several years. In a multiage atmosphere, differences become strengths instead of liabilities, and time is a friend.

Because greater variations in students' development exist in multiage than exist in single-grade groupings, students, teachers, and parents are forced to confront, accept, and build on each others' differences. If I want my children to resist peer pressure and media brainwashing, what better way to do it than for them to learn early that it's okay to be yourself, whether in reading "level," speaking poise, or physical development? And in a world battered by violence, political strife, and intolerance, it is so important that our children deal compassionately with each others' shortcomings and award generous and unenvying praise for each others' excellence.

Acceptance of self and others does not come overnight. For this reason, time is a great ally of the three-year program. Relationships often need to evolve gradually, and the security of a three-year space enhances their growth, facilitates bonding, and allows a healthy comraderie to take root and deepen.

But simply combining grade levels does not alone constitute a valid multiage grouping. Three more features are required: individual orientation; a family atmosphere; and parental involvement. These elements must go hand in hand with the embracement of differences and the benefits of time. While the above three features may appear in a single-grade classroom, when kneaded with multiage ingredients, the recipe produces a distinctly leavened rather than a flat loaf.

Individual orientation is perhaps the greatest benefit for multiage students. As every parent knows, two children from the same two parents will be markedly different people. Multiage has embraced both my daughters' different disposition traits and learning styles sensitively and effectively, because progress revolves around a child's own readiness.

My older daughter took off rapidly in her reading and writing growth. I recall vividly her utter delight and absorption in her first "chapter" book, *Squanto*, during her initial year with Penny and Jane. Penny had suggested the book to her, feeling that Christina was ready for it, and from there it was as though a rocket fuse had been lit. Even today Christina remembers how enthralled she was with her new passion, recalling that she chose to read her book rather than watch a movie with most of the rest of the class. While my younger daughter, Julianna, has followed a less steeply ascending flight path, she is equally happy with her book conquests, since they are right for her. Exemplifying her attitude is a remark she made to me recently: "Cricket [Christina] is having a growing spurt. I'm having a reading spurt!"

I have been so glad that on the one hand Christina didn't develop a love for reading by becoming a praise junkie motivated by comparison to fellow students at, below, or above "grade level." She learned to love reading for her own information and enjoyment. On the other hand, I've been pleased that Julianna has had no occasion to worry about whether she was learning to read fast enough. Each of my daughters has seen her fellow students reading materials ranging from six-word picture books to lengthy mysteries to thick nonfiction tomes.

As a classroom volunteer, I have also seen other students benefit consistently from this cherishing of individual progress. One particular student deserves mention here because I have had the advantage of working with her in two different multiage settings. In Jane and Penny's primary multiage I knew her as an enthusiastic but often overbearing and interruptive student whose writing and reading abilities were uneven. Had she been in a standardized single-grade classroom, her slow progress may have been painfully and detrimentally obvious. But since she was working at her own rate, her talents, instead of being choked, were allowed to blossom. While volunteering in the intermediate multiage class, I became better acquainted with her.

One time I led a discussion in her class on what killing and stealing really meant. We began by noting that our society has laws against such behavior. Next, I asked the students what other weapons existed besides guns, knives, bombs, etc. Some students expressed the idea that words could be weapons. Then up popped the hand of this student. She ventured that when we tell ourselves that we're a bad person or feel we're not good enough, our thoughts are like weapons against ourselves. That insightful comment catalyzed further discussion. The extended multiage time frame allowed me to notice this child's real gifts. I saw that she exhibited a highly developed sensitivity and grasp of deep concepts. This new awareness on my part alerted me to watch for her's and others' latent abilities.

Multiage's second important facet, the family atmosphere in which students thrive, rises naturally from our program's foundational accommodation to individual growth. Note that I use the pronoun *our* instead of *their* to refer to the multiage program. The program truly does belong to all of us.

Most parents consider their child's safety and well-being to be of paramount importance. They buy bicycle helmets, install smoke detectors, and make health-care appointments. Our society enacts laws requiring vehicles to stop for school buses, requires school air quality tests and building inspections, and opposes waste sites near schools. But what about emotional safety?

I remember the pit I felt in my stomach whenever I first thought of my older daughter's first day of kindergarten. I feared for my daughter's emotional well-being. Since then I have found the family atmosphere that develops in a multiage scenario to be a partial safety net for emotional danger. It helps provide in some measure "a home away from home."

During a daily "circle of friends" sharing time, I have seen children free enough to share painful events in their lives—a pet dying, parents divorcing, a parent moving out of state—and hopes for the purchase of a house enabling a father and child to live together instead of in a grandparent's home. As our society wrestles with changing family structures and practices, school more and more needs to be a place of security and dependable treatment. Multiage groups set a reliable stage on which trust and tolerance can develop.

As a family knows all too well, its members can exhibit certain grating traits. Nevertheless, these very foibles can strenthen family members even to the point of endearment. In a multiage setting founded on individual respect and fortified by a three-year time frame, students grow in acceptance of each others' "negative" sides and come to discover, recognize, and cherish the "positive" attributes existing in everyone.

Two instances come to mind. One child I have worked with as a volunteer leader in Literature Groups and Communication Workshops needs a lot of specific approval. She wants her contributions to receive extra special attention, almost to the point of irritation. Recently this child raised her hand and made a derogatory comment on a literature group member's enactment of a harmonica player. The remark was treated with instant dismissal from Jane, firmly but without condemnation: "We don't do put downs in this class." What interested me was to see the potentially damaging behavior diffused so quickly and decisively, and how the incident passed by with the kind of distinct message a family rule would convey, "Oh, our family just doesn't do that." And because fellow students knew the child commenting and were familiar with her personality, the effect of the comment was less damaging. Just as a family might say,"Oh, that's just Uncle Horace's way," the class accepted this child. A family may wince some at his behavior, but because he is Uncle Horace, they can understand and love him on some level. Individual children are welcomed in a similar way in a multiage class.

A second child who provides an example of multiage familial benefits has been in the program for three years. Both of my children have been in class with her. This child has an alert and questioning mind, but she can also behave thoughtlessly and disruptively. Not long ago I heard one of my daughters remark to the other, "You know I really do like X. She can be really irritating, but she can be really funny, too. I have fun playing with her sometimes." If my child had had only one year to develop a relationship with this child, it would have been much more difficult to achieve that feeling of friendship. Her initial assessment of that child had been definitely negative.

A multiage family-like setup also enhances social adjustment. One example is my older daughter's increased comfort level and friendship with boys. Due to having no male siblings, making male friends has been an important and needed step for her. An easygoing, brotherly relationship with the boys in her group has emerged. Her teachers certainly have given attention to healthy attitudes regarding friendship, and their efforts are supported by the children and parents who make up the multiage family. Friendships are strengthened by having three years in which to develop.

Another helpful side of multiage participation that relates to a family-like climate is the opportunity for students to assume the roles of an older or younger sibling. Just as a younger child would ask a bigger sister or brother for help, my younger daughter has been able to look to older students for assistance in editing and writing stories. Recently, she was excited about writing a story on some holiday activities she'd had. She began with a burst of sentences in her day book, but she soon became wearied of finishing. The abundance of her ideas far surpassed her writing stamina. Her frustration occurred on my day to help with Communications Workshop, and she expressed her concerns to me. I suggested she might like to take a rest for that day and do another section the next day. She reluctantly agreed, but I could see she was not really satisfied with that solution.

An interesting resolution followed. The next day she came home from school exultant, "Mom, I finished my story!" When I congratulated her and asked how she had done so much writing, she responded, "Oh, it was easy. X helped me spell all the hard words!" What a lovely example of "sisterly" nurturing and support!

The final aspect of a multiage family atmosphere I have noted is the sense of belonging it gives. My children enjoy a loyalty to their classmates and teachers that is in some ways comparable to the bond akin to a surname identity. One might sum up this group connection or community sense by utilizing a mathematical sentence, with each component of the equation a necessary ingredient: Family atmosphere + time = secure individuals + community.

One hears much talk today touting the benefits of increased parent involvement in our educational systems. Multiage programs provide a golden opportunity, perhaps even a mandate, for parental closeness to a child's education. I have grown so much by having responsibility for and a concomitant ownership in children's classes. By fostering this feeling of increased connectedness, our home and school spheres have become symbiotic, concentric rather than merely overlapping.

Most parents contribute readily. From the program's inception, we have been asked each September to write down goals for our child. This made it immediately clear to me as a parent that my views mattered and that I was expected to have some! No parental pass-offs, mental abdication, or check-out scanning of children here. In addition, periodic surveys come home all year soliciting from parents feelings and ideas on what works well or needs improvement. I have found these vehicles to be an excellent way to communicate my concerns.

For example, I remember in my younger daughter's first year, I began to feel concerned that she might be developing poor and inefficient habits forming letters, and that she might need more guidance. Not only were my comments taken receptively, but also immediate action occurred. As always, my thoughts were valued and welcomed.

The scheduling of parent conferences is yet another concrete example indicative of the program's tone of individual respect for parents as well as students. Instead of alloting fifteen-minute slots all packed into one day, à la "take a number" deli department style, parents enjoy a conference arranged for a leisurely and convenient time. Longer conferences allow for a thoughtful interchange of ideas to occur. They encourage parents to really "open up" about any problems and for parents and teachers to get to know each other better as human beings.

The luxury of the cumulative three-year element of the multiage setting adds to the quality of the parent/teacher relationship. I have found that I am able to genuinely regard my children's teachers as friends, in a cooperative and mutually productive manner. It is a friendship reminiscent of the link that people have to their small-town general store keeper, as opposed to the casual acquaintance one has with a supermarket cashier.

Besides experiencing easy communication with teachers, parents of multiage students tend to feel an ownership in their children's education. The teachers invite true participation from parents, not just observation or peripheral activity in the classroom. I get involved with the multiage classes through my weekly Literature Group session, Communication Workshop assistance, and song sessions. Taking advantage of these opportunities, as well as the classes' "drop in anytime" policy, really have given me stock in my daughters' school world and motivated me to keep its dividends paying.

At my children's school, parental ownership is not confined to only classroom opportunities. It stems as well from abundant provisions made for parental immersion in activities such as field trips, special workshops arranged for sharing parental talents and interests, story typing, weekly newsletter updates, and, of course, the pumpkin project outings to name just a few.

Since parents and families are so closely included in the multiage scene, they get to know each other more readily. I feel as if all the students are to some extent "my" kids. I have made several lovely friendships with other parents because I didn't just see them occasionally, but repeatedly. And, since I know I'll see them again the next year and the next, I am more likely to invest some effort in those relationships. I even think a spillover effect occurs from the multiage embracing of differences. Parents are less wary and judgmental of each other, and that can't hurt!

Due to my sustained attachment to our program right from its first year, I have witnessed its progressive evolution and steady improvement each year. Yes, we encounter turbulence every so often, but a multiage classroom's strength can weather it. And because of the program's structural integrity, durability, and flexibility, my children are becoming more confident, active learners, taking more and more responsibility in guiding their own educations.

The past four years have expanded, challenged, and uplifted my vision of school and learning. After all, isn't the purpose of education to lead us and our children out from our self-confines and into the world around us? I have learned that simply combining grade levels does not constitute a true or functioning multiage classroom. Successful multiage grouping needs the underlying and singular components of embracing differences and providing time, combined with the three characteristics of individual orientation, familial climate, and parental commitment. Thus equipped, the multiage classroom powers a unique vehicle for learning that has helped wing my family upward.

References

BULLA, CLYDE ROBERT. 1954. *Squanto: Friend of the Pilgrims.* New York: Scholastic.

Safe and Successful

9

Emotionally Disturbed Children in the Multiage Setting

Kathy McDonough and Katie Johnson

The Knight Children's Center is one of the nine programs of the New England Home For Little Wanderers. The home has been around for just over 125 years. Established and named shortly after the Civil War, it began as an orphanage for the many children left parentless by that war. We have evolved as society has changed, and we are now a residential treatment center for children ages five through twelve. We operate on the principle of providing schooling in a therapeutic milieu. The children that come through our doors have emotional and behavioral difficulties because they have been severely traumatized, often as victims of physical, sexual, and/or drug abuse, sometimes by being a witness to loved ones being abused. No wonder they couldn't concentrate on school activities! Some of our students are day students and attend only our school program. Others live in our residence from five to seven days a week and are either in the process of becoming adopted or working towards being able to live at home safely.

Our students have spent years failing in public school. Most, if not all, of our students haven't and couldn't thrive in large public school classrooms that, compared to us, are unstructured. The kids were often physically or verbally abusive towards classmates, adults, or themselves: attacking teachers, lighting fires, or attempting to harm themselves. Many children who behaved in these ways had been hospitalized in psychiatric wards and so missed more schooling. Once they have made it to us, they must find safety and success. Our whole program is committed to helping them do just this.

"What's your word today, Terisa?"

Silence. Terisa's eyes welled up with tears and she pulled back even further from the teacher.

"I know it's hard coming into a new school in the middle of the year. It's scary not to know the teachers or have any friends yet. Maybe you can think of a word you would like me to write on your card today," Kathy, the teacher, said.

Terisa caught her breath and stopped crying just long enough to blurt out "happy." Kathy printed the letters on a narrow oaktag card while she refrained from commenting about how Terisa sure didn't look very happy.

Terisa's seventh birthday was in a few weeks. It was her third day in a new class in a new school, and she had refused to do any work until now. "Happy" was Terisa's first word, her entry into literacy.

At the round table Karl and Randy, both nine, were co-authoring a book about dirt bikes. They had been working on this piece for a week, taking turns dictating while the other wrote. They were busy describing all the neat things a dirt bike could do, like going up ramps and popping wheelies, and writing them into their piece.

Sheri, seven, was writing her umpteenth piece about *The Little Mermaid*. When she came to a word she couldn't spell, Sheri would ask the air, "How do you spell *Triton*?" Martin, at eight, the most proficient writer, would often lift his pencil off his paper for a second, spell the word for her out loud, then zip his pencil along to finish his draft. Kathy kept encouraging Martin to write words for Sheri in her personal spelling dictionary, so she'd have them for future use, but Kathy understood when he didn't take the time to do it. She couldn't blame him for wanting as many seconds of his precious writing period as possible all for himself. He always seemed to have a million ideas that he just had to get down on paper.

Shane, nearly ten, sat alone at his desk by the window, looking at a Polaroid picture of his new puppy at home. Shane would call home each night to ask what new thing his puppy learned today. He spent a lot of time thinking, thinking, thinking of the shortest sentence he could possibly write, using only words he was sure of spelling. Shane hated writing and didn't see much purpose in school either. He put a lot of energy into trying to show that he knew everything and never needed any help. Perhaps, Kathy often thought, he needed the most help.

Hank, one of the most volatile of the children in this group, the Scouts class, had a beatific smile, smiling through even his worst blowouts. Even Hank, though, never came apart during writing time. Dark brows knit together, lips moving silently, he was concentrating now on catching all the periods in his story about taking his sister to the park on his last visit home.

This was a typical morning's writing time in our school's second-youngest class. Terisa was still six, soon to be seven, and Shane was turning ten in the fall. Our school has been multiage for years, but we didn't know it.

Multiage is in our history, in our bones, part of the structure of our school. Each August our principal sits down and lists the names of all fifty-three of our students in the order of their ages. She then divides that list into six multiage classroom groups. Groups are reformed each year; the span of ages in each group varies.

One way to ensure success is to be ungraded, so we are an ungraded school made up of six classrooms. Each classroom has a name— Pumpkins, Scouts, Comets, Hobbits, Superstars, and Rangers, youngest to oldest. Students of various ages work together in the same class at very different levels, all with different teacher expectations, all learning. Simply being placed in ungraded classrooms is one way our children are given a positive school life. School work is also not graded. Work is often hands-on. When it does involve worksheets, no *X*'s are used, in red or any color. Only correct marks, smiling faces, and stickers are placed on each child's paper. Four times a year a written summary of the child's performance goes to the parents, or to the agency that has custody of the child. Traditional report cards have no value here, but our curriculum is as similar to that of public schools as we can appropriately make it. Students know that they are placed in a class because of age, not because they were promoted for academic or behavioral success. This way they can not get held back—that is, fail again—because they didn't do well in school.

Usually the three youngest classrooms have quite a wide range of ages, this year five through eight, seven through nine, and eight through eleven. The setup of our classrooms compliments multiage/multi-level teaching. Each class has no more than eleven students, and each class has two teachers, one an assistant, usually a recent college graduate. Very few whole-class discussion lessons are presented each day, due to the nature of our students. Poor peer skills, distractibility, easy frustration, and rage are high on the list for lesson interference. Because of these, we more often teach in small groups than in full groups, even though the full groups are not large. Each room's team of teachers plans constantly for the variety of student needs. In whole-class lessons, often one teacher presents while the other floats around helping students.

The Comets class, ages eight through eleven, are learning about life cycles for this year's science fair. They have fertile eggs in an incubator and chrysalides in a terrarium. Each morning at nine, as the children trickle in, each stops at the incubator and the terrarium. They look and ask, "Have they hatched yet?" Karl takes out his science log and draws what he sees. Peter and Randy, instead of drawing, write lengthy log entries. A little later in the morning, after Sustained Silent Reading, the science lesson begins. The teacher, Toni, uses a variety of approaches within a half-hour to meet the needs of all the students. The class starts by reviewing facts they have learned about chicken eggs.

Toni holds a basket filled with colored plastic eggs that break in half. Inside each egg is a slip of paper with a question about chickens written on it. The students take turns picking an egg and opening it.

Toni adeptly arranges who will read and answer each question. Peter, an excellent reader, chooses an egg with a fairly easy question. Toni asks Karl, who is sitting next to Peter and is in the early stages of literacy acquisition, to read the question and have Peter answer it.

Zachary, the newest and youngest student in the class, is having a hard time concentrating on anything yet, and a hard time remembering some of the facts. When Sheri opens an egg with the question, "What is the hard, white, outer covering of an egg called?" the teacher sees Zachary's hand fly up into the air, nearly lifting him off of his seat. She calls on Zachary to answer. This is the one fact he always knows.

"A shell !" he blurts out, and as he sits back a big smile comes over his face. The plastic egg review goes on until everyone has had a chance to open, read, and answer a question, all carefully and quickly arranged by Toni to ensure individual success for each child.

Next, Toni talks to the whole class about how the children will care for the chicks in the classroom once they hatch, and how the chicks will need a certain kind of food, a brooder, and water. She talks about how the children should handle the animals, and finally reminds them that the chicks will be taken to a farm after they are two weeks old. To help the younger and the less focused students get through the lesson, she gives each one a vocabulary word to be responsible for. Karl is handed an index card with "brooder" written on it.

At the end of the discussion students are asked to write about how to care for the chicks. The expectation is that they each write something, and they do, but the outcome is as varied as the students. Jahmad takes lined composition paper and begins to write. Later he draws a sketch that he staples to his writing. Jahmad includes everything the teacher spoke of. Zachary takes a piece of large drawing paper with a line at the bottom. He asks for help and writes, "The chicks need clean water." Zachary spends the rest of the time drawing a picture of a chicken. Kareem does his part by writing two sentences. Then, while everyone else is writing or drawing, Kareem looks through the books in the classroom.

The oldest class, the Rangers, have math workshop. Math workshop, consisting of hands-on lessons for constantly shifting small groups, occurs two times a week for each student. Kristin and Amanda, the teachers, look at the skills their students need and plan workshops to meet them. The students' groupings are not always the same. For example, if Matt, Jamie, and Mariel need to learn to make change from a dollar, they will be called to a money workshop with Kristin and then given individual practice. Meanwhile Amanda might be working on exponents with Adam and Garrett. While these teacher-directed groups are in progress, the other students, not currently in a focused group, work independently in math workbooks or on games, puzzles, and other activities from the math box. On another day, it may be Tami, Jamie, and Lonny who need to work on long division, while Adam and Matt do some estimating together with Amanda.

Students from the Hobbits, Superstars, or Rangers occasionally tutor the younger children, sometimes to help the teacher out, usually as a self-esteem booster for the older student. Last year Garrett, a Ranger, came to the Scouts' math class every Thursday to work with a student named Sheri. He would help her finish a worksheet, play a math game or help her practice addition and subtraction facts with flashcards. Henry, from the same older class, came and read a book every Wednesday to another student, Karl. Sometimes they would then draw a picture together about a favorite part.

Sometimes, particularly in the Superstars and Rangers, the ability range is so incredibly great that some of the children change rooms for reading and science groups, so that more levels can be accommodated by the four teachers in those rooms. Lori, the Superstars' head teacher, has a group of four readers who met one day when Katie Johnson, a visiting literacy consultant, was there. For these four, the ages ranged from ten to twelve years, but their reading abilities were closer to grades second through fourth. Lori and Katie sat around the circular table with the students, Howie, Tami, Mary, and Julio, each with a book.

"I can start off by telling you about the book I've just finished—it's called *Walking Trees*," said Katie. "It's about a teacher who teaches writing to kids."

"That's because that's what you do, too," chimed in Tami understandingly.

"And what have you been reading lately?" Katie smiled invitingly around the circle.

"I haven't read anything," Howie answered quickly, and in instant response came Lori's voice, in determined contradiction.

"Howie, of course you have," Lori remonstrated. "Remember that mystery we were reading together last week?"

"No," said Howie, his normal dimples deepened into potholes by the anxiety-producing question. "But here's this one. I looked at this today," he added, holding up *The Giving Tree*.

"Did you like looking at that one?" Katie asked, and at Howie's smile she continued. "Good, Howie, please be thinking about how you'd tell someone why you liked it while we find out what everyone else has read." She turned to Tami.

"How about you, Tami? You've been listening so well, tell us what book you have."

"It's a mystery about this girl in an attic," Tami responded promptly. "This girl, see, she goes to the store and then she meets her friend and then. . . ."

Katie stopped her about five sentences into this summary. "That's a great choice, Tami, you sure know a lot about that book."

"And then, see, the girl finds out that there is a secret room. . . ."

"Can you hold on to the rest of it for a minute, Tami, while we find out about the others around the table?" She lowered her voice to a stage whisper. "It's important to leave people a little bit in suspense, you know, so they'll want to read it too."

Tami swallowed, hard, all those words she was about to say, and graciously assented, with a conspiratorial look. "Sure, that's fine," she said.

Julio, after impatiently informing us that he'd been ready to talk for the past half an hour, spat out the name. "*Freckle Juice*. It's good." He turned quickly to Mary. "Your turn."

"It's hard to choose—I've been reading a lot of books lately . . . but . . ." Mary turned over a well-used volume of the *Babysitters Club* series. "This one."

"Well," Lori gave a little laugh, "I've been reading a book about planning weddings." She stopped.

"Oh!" exclaimed Katie. "Because you're getting married this summer, right?"

Lori laughed again. "Well, it's an interesting book, I've learned some things I didn't know before." Tami, the world-wise twelve-year-old, looked at Lori hard, as if she was expecting more.

"Well anyway," Katie went on, "I want to tell you a little about this book *Walking Trees*. It's written by Ralph Fletcher, and it's about how he teaches a lot of kids in New York City, city kids just like you all are, how to do writing. He has some good times and some bad times—I think the kids there aren't as nice to writing teachers as you kids are to me and Lori. I liked it, though, because he does some of the same things I do with writing and it made me feel good to read it."

She paused. "Now I've told you about my book, and I've tried to tell you three things about it." She held up her fingers. "First, I told you the name of the book and the author; second, I told you a little about what it was about; and third, I told you why I liked it." She touched each finger as she listed the three things.

"I don't think that's a book for kids," said Julio impatiently. Julio, at ten the youngest one in the group, is almost always impatient.

Lori gave a chortle.

"You're probably right, Julio," said Katie. "If I were going to choose one of the people at this table to tell about this book, who would it be?" She glanced around at the group.

Howie pointed at Lori, and immediately Tami did too.

"I think so, too," Katie said. "Why would I think Lori might be interested in this book, Howie?"

"Because she's a teacher, too, and she teaches us writing. When you're not here," he added generously.

"Good thinking, that makes sense to me, too," Katie agreed. "So when I am telling a friend about a book I need to think about my audience. So if you share some things about your book with a friend, you need to think about what the friend might like to hear. Who can remember what three things I told you about my book?"

"The name of it," replied Tami promptly.

"And something about it, you know, what it's about," said Julio quickly.

"But not everything about it," added Tami, "you want it to be suspicious—is that the word?" She shook her head. "No—you know that word, so the person will want to read it?"

"Good remembering, Tami," Katie said. "Suspenseful, you mean?"

"Right," said Tami. "Make what you tell about it suspenseful."

"And tell why you liked it, how it connected to you some way," Lori said.

"Great. Now we'll each get a piece of paper and write to someone at this table about the book we've been reading." They each took a piece from the stack Lori placed on the table and took a pencil out of the pencil can. "How about if we just do it in a circle, the way we're sitting here. Howie, you write to me, I'll write to Lori, Lori will write to Tami, and on around."

"So I'll write to Mary," Tami continued, "and Mary will write to Julio, and—who will you write to, Julio?" she asked.

Julio stabbed the air toward Howie. "Him."

"Is it gonna be like a letter?" Howie asked.

"Yes," Katie answered. "Dear Katie, yours has to start."

The dimples deepened. The pencils began to move over the papers. We all wrote to each other for seven minutes solid.

At our school, the choice of reading material and responsibility for that choice is always given to the students. There are no basal readers here. Choice is important in our setting for both success in building self-esteem among fragile readers and for safety, to avoid power struggles. Perhaps choices are not as broad as in public school, but we feel that the choices are well planned and purposely limited to maintain some control. For this population of children, controlled choice equals safety.

"For the second half of reading time, do you want to work on your rhyming puzzle or shall I read to you?" The Scouts' teacher might ask.

"Do you want to work with cubes or sticks?" Kelley might ask her class, the Pumpkins.

We offer planned control through choice, because in our setting, having no control can equal chaos and bring a child to unbearable anxiety.

During the writing period at the beginning of each day, the Scouts begin with structured choice. Today Kathy, their teacher, says to them, "When I call on you, choose a partner to read with." The children choose a partner and read their own pieces to each other and give each other compliments. "I like the way you made the car red and black," Ken says to Randy. "Thanks," replies Randy. This is part of the routine, too. Sometimes Kathy hears them laughing, so she knows the compliments are genuine. "That's so funny, that part about the dragon catching squirrels," Sam said to Hank one day. First choosers get to go to the square table, later pairs move their chairs. "We haven't had the table for a long time," Sheri said the other day—these children, like children everywhere, keep track of their teachers.

Although we provide a choice of what and whom to work with, there is almost no choice of where to be. Belonging to the group and having a "home" room is very important here, partly because of the fragmented nature of the children's backgrounds, but also because the work they do in their home rooms is only part of the program at the Knight Children's Center. Every child has therapist appointments weekly, many have other therapy sessions with their parents. Some, probably one-third, go to the two resource room teachers regularly for one-to-one remedial help in math and reading. The classes go to the art studio twice a week and to the gym for structured physical education. The family atmosphere of the home room provides a secure place for each child to come back to.

The art and physical education curricula are being coordinated more and more with the reading and writing the children are doing. When the Hobbits got hooked recently on Aardema's *Why Mosquitoes Buzz in People's Ears*, the children read it to the art teachers who responded with a plan to create mobiles of the characters. This integrated project kept growing, moving back and forth between reading and writing and art and movement, for several weeks.

Integrating curriculum across the classrooms and integrating children so that they can learn to work together are two of the goals of our school. We are not multiage on purpose, but multiage comes from our structure and contributes to the main goal of keeping children safe. And *do* we keep them safe and give them success? The cold statistics say yes. Another measure comes from the warm responses of the children themselves. For the yearbook, Kathy asked the kids to supply thank-yous for the staff, as a surprise dedication.

"Thank you," Jamie wrote, "for teaching me reading and writing."

Tim said, "Thank you for helping me work out problems with my family."

"For your understanding," Tami wrote. "And sense of tivity."

And Martin, simply: " Thank you for keeping me safe."

References

AARDEMA, VERNA. 1975. *Why Mosquitoes Buzz in People's Ears: A West African Tale*. New York: Dial Press.

BLUME, JUDY. 1971. *Freckle Juice*. New York: Four Winds Press.

FLETCHER, RALPH. 1991. *Walking Trees: Teaching Teachers in the New York City Schools*. Portsmouth, NH: Heinemann.

SILVERSTEIN, SHEL. 1964. *The Giving Tree*. New York: Harper & Row.

From Multiage to Multiple Ways of Knowing

Discovering the Strengths of Our Children

Jean Anne Clyde

In 1990, the state of Kentucky enacted the Kentucky Education Reform Act (KERA), a piece of legislation designed to rid its schools of the inequities that historically had existed. Based upon the latest research on children, learning, and teaching, this sweeping reform package put forth new expectations regarding the kinds of educational experiences considered appropriate for young children. Developmentally appropriate practice, local governance of schools, and a commitment to including parents as partners in education were all a part of the law. But the most controversial aspect of KERA was its emphasis on "continuous progress," and the corresponding call for non-graded, or multiage, classrooms for primary children.

Because multiage classrooms have been mandated, there is a good deal of fear among those Kentucky teachers who for years have organized their curricula around a tidy schedule of distinct subjects. Grade-specific teachers' manuals, not individual instincts or understandings about learning, have long governed teachers' decision-making. Still, many of the teachers acknowledge that each year a few children whose lack of experience or inability to make sense of school, or whose views of the world are incompatible with the constraints operating within the classroom context, have "fallen through the cracks." Clearly, those practices have not always served children well.

Concerned with the challenges that a class of seven-, eight-, *or* nine-year-olds presents, many teachers are overwhelmed at the thought of blending these groups. It is not the children's ages that pose the problem, however; rather, it is the multiple abilities implied by those ages. Because few of Kentucky's teachers have seen or experienced multiage classrooms, it is difficult for them to envision the benefits. Teachers are wondering: With so much diversity, how many *more* children are destined to fall through the cracks?

I would like to argue that it is the lens through which we view our children that complicates our attempts to support them in a multiage setting. Historically, we have relied primarily on judgments about their language abilities (their reading, writing, and talking) and their ability to "do math" in determining what children "know" and understand. Yet verbal and mathematical performances provide only partial evidence of what young children know (Eisner 1982; Gardner 1983; Harste, Woodward & Burke 1984). In his book, *Cognition and Curriculum* (1982), Elliott Eisner suggests that in restricting the ways our children can demonstrate what they know, we are also imposing restrictions on what they can learn.

These ideas begin to make more sense when we think about the children whom we have taught. Each of us probably remembers a child who loved to draw, whose journal was decorated with the characters he or she had invented, and the actions that revealed who those characters were. Unfortunately, we may have viewed our young artists' "work" as evidence of distraction, as "off-task" behavior. In many ways, such failure to fully appreciate what these young artists were trying to do was a reflection of society's failure to value non-linguistic endeavors. Art, music, and physical education often have been considered "frills," and are often the first subjects to be eliminated when budget cuts loom. Furthermore, the mainstream curriculum has offered few opportunities for children to explore talents, abilities, and strategies for learning in these non-linguistic ways.

What might happen if we allowed or even encouraged our young artists to use art to convey what they know, if we valued art as a form of communication? What if we were to broaden the curriculum so that rather than using only language to learn and to demonstrate what they know, children were invited to use art, music, drama, or movement as tools for thinking, as vehicles for sharing understandings? Is it possible that by inviting children to *choose* their forms of expression, teachers could develop more insights for working with children with a wide range of differences and abilities in multiage settings?

These were the questions I was asking when I returned to the classroom as a co-teacher in a first-grade class. The next year, the classroom became multiage, and I was able to remain with half (twelve) of "my" kids a second year in a research capacity as I continued to try to find answers to those questions. During those two years, one young child, six-year-old Douglas, did more to push my thinking regarding the potential of an expanded view of curriculum than any of the theorists whose work I had read. Through observing Douglas hard at work, I came to understand the role that art can play in thinking and learning.

Douglas was a little guy when he began first grade, the youngest and the smallest of his classmates. He was giggly and wiggly and active, and one of the wildest storytellers I'd ever heard. Just listen as Douglas tells one of his "scary stories."

> Well, um, Momma has to leave to go to work, and the little boy stayed home. He was thirteen years old. And then this ghost came out an' he was floatin' down the wall, and then he was sittin' there watchin' TB and den the ghost got under the seat and da monster was hidin' and, um, and then the ghost went, "Boo!" and then, and then he got home, and then he eatin'. Instead he came and picked up Mom, and that's the end. (Transcribed from a videotape from October 1990)

As one might imagine, there was always much squinting among those of us who were trying desperately to make sense of Douglas's stories. This was true for his written work, as well, which was also difficult to access. While I always believed that Douglas understood what he was trying to convey, both oral and written language seemed to pose problems for him. It was months later when I discovered why.

Language requires an "author" to organize his or her thinking sequentially, in a logical order, if it is to be understood. Douglas was a child who had no shortage of wonderful ideas, yet this demand for linearity seemed unwieldy for him. Determining ways to support his growth and help him feel successful as a learner, as mandated by KERA, posed a significant challenge to his teachers.

In mid-January, 1991, in an effort to provide a new opportunity for children to write for an authentic audience, we instituted the *Allstar Update*, a classroom newspaper published by the children for themselves, their families, and their friends. Children determined the kinds of columns that would be included, and they filled out applications for positions of their choosing. Douglas, who had returned from Christmas vacation with an itch to play basketball, applied to be a sportswriter, and he was "hired." His contribution to the publication was an illustration of a game in progress. When he had completed his piece, Douglas met with his friend Andy to confer about it.

The boys were well into their conversation when I stopped by to see how things were going. Much to my surprise, the basketball "game" was still being played—on paper—as the boys talked about the picture (see Figure 10-1). I watched as Douglas drew a player, then drew a second ball to indicate a shift in "possession." His attention shifted from the goal to another player, then back to the ball again. These shifts seemed to parallel those he made during storytelling; but in the context of language, his shifts had been much more difficult to follow. Interestingly, while working on his illustration, Douglas's shifts seemed to

Figure 10-1

enhance his message, not confuse it. During this fascinating conference, Douglas displayed for Andy and me how he was discovering the usefulness of art in organizing his thinking. Rather than being trapped by the constraints of language that so frustrated both him and his audience, Douglas approached his illustration, or "text," more globally. At last he had discovered a medium that supported his storytelling.

Within two weeks of Douglas's experience as a published "sportswriter," his concern for basketball seemed to fade and a new sport—skateboard riding—began to dominate his interests. Rather than simply talking about the sport, Douglas began using his art to explore his favorite pastime. Gone were his longtime struggles to "get something down on paper." Instead, he wisely chose his journal as the place to explore his interest in skateboarding, a topic that otherwise would have had no place in school. He took that journal with him wherever he went.

Each day Douglas devoted every spare moment to producing loopy little skateboard riders in his journal. At first his intense work baffled me. Yet given his unshakable focus, I was convinced that he was learning something that was of vital importance to him.

A conversation with Douglas in mid-February confirmed my suspicions. After sharing several of his latest entries, Douglas offered to draw some skateboard riders for me. First he produced a large arc, a ramp that his figure would ride on; next he added one of his men, perched on the board close to the top of the ramp (see Figure 10-2). After he had drawn his figure, Douglas paused and carefully examined his drawing, squinching his eyes up as though reviewing a mental image. After nearly a minute, he announced that his picture was "not right." As he erased the arms on his figure, Douglas explained, "Cause he be lookin' like he's goin' down." He was right; no skateboard rider would have remained on a board if he held his arms as Douglas had originally placed them. He quickly revised his drawing, repositioning the arms. Still dissatisfied with the image, he continued with his story, providing a play-by-play of the action that unfolded on the paper, using multiple images (Hubbard 1989) to represent those actions (see Figure 10-3). As I watched Douglas throughout this intense inquiry, I realized that his keen interest in drawing had nothing to do with becoming an artist. Instead, representing his experience through two-dimensional drawings

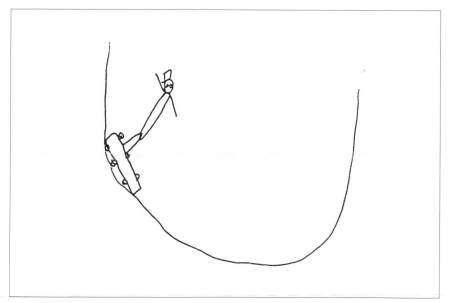

Figure 10–2

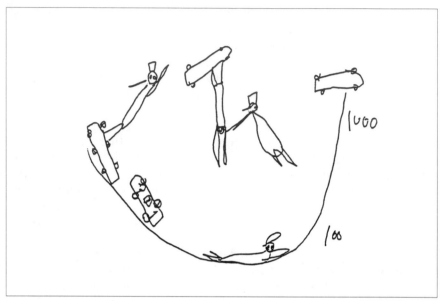

Figure 10–3

allowed him to rethink and revise his understandings of the physics of skateboard riding so that he could improve his own mastery of the sport. In the process, Douglas was using art to help him to think like a physicist and an athlete.

We have long heard about the value of oral and written language as tools for learning (Barnes 1992; Watson & Young 1986; Wells 1986; Wells & Chang-Wells, 1992), but few have argued for the intellectual benefits of art. However, through his diligent efforts to become a better skateboard rider, Douglas helped me to understand the potential role of art in learning.

By December of 1991, the child who one year earlier had experienced much defeat in communicating through language was revered by his classmates—young and old—as the class artist. So much had transpired in fifteen months! Working with Douglas a second year had provided us the time needed to fully understand his strengths, his interests, and the critical role that art played in his learning. How easy it had been for Douglas his second year! Rather than devoting energy to understanding the rules and expectations of a new classroom context, he entered his second year confident and secure knowing that half of his classmates and his teacher understood who he was. The child who by conventional measures represented the most difficult challenge within a multiage setting had become successful, making contributions to the classroom that were honored and acknowledged. Within a more traditional classroom, with less time for teachers and students to know Douglas and to understand him, and where a single lens would have been used to determine what he knew, Douglas would have been destined to become one of the children who fell through the cracks.

The multiage setting and the expanded curriculum supported Douglas's younger peers as well. I noted how much easier it was for them to become a part of the strong community that already existed than it had been for previous students to establish a community of learners in other years. There were so many demonstrations of how to go about learning available, so many talents valued, such wonderful social support, and so many knowledgeable friends from whom they could seek advice. They soon felt as secure as Douglas had come to feel.

Throughout that year, as I continued my investigation of children's knowing, the teacher and I collaborated on ways to expand the curriculum to invite children's strengths to emerge. What did these children know? What were they good at? What did they care about? Answers to these questions gained importance as we considered the diverse interests and experiences of this multiage group.

Exploring Multiple Ways of Knowing Through "Choice Time"

One of the most natural ways to uncover what children knew seemed to be to organize the room into "areas" that contained different kinds of supplies and tools. Into each day was built "Choice Time," two forty-five-minute blocks of time during which children signed up and worked in areas to create, to investigate, to learn. To an onlooker used to more traditional classrooms, the children's work might have appeared little more than play. However, it was largely through these open-ended invitations for children to create their own curricular experiences that their individual strengths, their interests, and their current understandings of the world were made readily visible.

Observations of these multiage children at work using a variety of different media provided important information about who they were, as well as the kinds of experiences that they found naturally intriguing. One morning while working at the sand table, Leslie, Cameron, Matthew, and Jamar discovered the glittery quality that sand displayed when allowed to spill slowly through the sunlight. "It looks shimmery, like water," Leslie remarked, as they watched it sift through their fingers. Their discovery led the group to co-create a landscape at the sand table that would contain a "real waterfall." They carefully crafted the sand into a land form that resembled the buttes found in the southwest

United States. There was much discussion among this cross-aged group about the height the banks should be, and a great deal of experimentation regarding how to create a lake that would capture the water once it spilled off the top of their "mountain." The group intensely studied the trail the water formed as it splashed, then meandered, through the sand below it. Their experimentation drew much attention when they talked about it during sharing time.

On another day, seven-year-old Robert and his two six-year-old friends, Katherine and Richard, investigated animal artifacts in the science area. What began as a play using hand puppets evolved into a drama in which the boys were "scientists who take care of animals," and Katherine became an injured cheetah with a broken leg. As the action unfolded, Richard paused to "take an X-ray" of the animal's leg. He quickly sketched a picture of a bone with what appeared to be a break in it. "Here is the X-ray of this cheetah," he announced, handing the drawing to his friends. Then, pointing to the specific problem area, he informed them, "*Here* is the disconnections." When the boys had finished their work on the cheetah, Richard produced a second X-ray. "Look at her leg now. It's cured." The self-generated X-ray confirmed Richard's assessment.

Six-year-old Ben and seven-year-old Cameron decided to work together to design a habitat for a house cat. Using a shoe box for their setting, the boys created a small cat, which they mounted on the end of a popsicle stick so they could move it around. Taking into consideration their feline's needs, they created a tiny mouse, which they also mounted on a stick. They considered the needs of their mouse as well, by poking a tiny hole in the side of their box that was large enough for their mouse to get through, but too small for the cat.

"Jean Anne, do you know why we made our mouse so small?" Cameron asked me as I watched them working.

"No, why?" I asked.

"Well, look at the size of our cat," Cameron suggested. The size of the two animals was no accident; the boys had carefully considered proportional size in creating the characters for their habitat.

These stories provide just a glimpse at the innovation that permeated Choice Time each day. Children worked productively together, self-selecting groups and partners on the basis of shared interests rather than age. They consistently created thought-provoking challenges for themselves, and during Sharing Time they talked about their decision-making and the problems that arose in the process. Their ideas encouraged us to incorporate similar kinds of experiences into our planned curriculum.

Beyond Choice Time: Incorporating Multiple Ways of Knowing into the Curriculum

The "how-tos" of broadening the curriculum to include other "ways of knowing" remains a slippery idea for many. The story that follows provides one example of how a theme study can be broadened to include other ways of thinking about and understanding a topic, and documents the impact on primary children of expanding the curriculum.

In March, the children began an in-depth study of Inuit Indians. Their questions about the clothing, food, and lifestyles of our northern neighbors were naturally included. They also inquired about the culture's music and rhythms. Children were invited to listen to Inuit music and to create instruments so that they could experiment with the music for themselves. This investigation so captivated Douglas (now a second-year student) and his friend Jamar that they initiated a self-study of how to produce the rhythms that characterized the music. Gradually their inquiries led to their independent investigation of rhythms found in their *own* African American culture and to their intense study of the science of musical sound. These two children, who previously had experienced such difficulty sharing meaning linguistically, had discovered a comfortable medium through which to communicate with their peers.

They began bringing in cardboard boxes of all sizes, taping each corner securely so that it could withstand the continual experimentation that took place each morning during the forty-five minutes of Choice Time they devoted to their "music." Their teacher introduced books on percussion instruments, and they soon learned a vocabulary that enabled them to communicate about the sounds they were producing, discussing bass, snare, bongo, other percussion instruments, and their sounds with great accuracy. Within a few short weeks, they were producing syncopated rhythms that powerfully invited their friends to move and dance along.

Jamar and Douglas were eager to share their daily compositions, and played each morning to a receptive audience of their multiaged peers. As the boys became more informed about how to "make music," they provided constant demonstrations to their peers of how to play their "instruments" and how to produce two complementary rhythms that were engaging to listeners. They even began experimenting with the impact of dynamics (playing loud and soft) on the effectiveness of their pieces.

Soon they were joined by others, both same-aged and younger peers, interested in the production of such interesting and impressive rhythms. The boys worked patiently with their friends, demonstrating how to play and directing the non-stop activity that occurred each day.

Georgette, a voracious reader from a very affluent family, joined the boys daily. I smiled at her initial attempts at making music, observing that at first she appeared as challenged by producing rhythms as the boys were by literacy. Yet her performances were understandable; even though Georgette was learning to play piano, she lacked experience with the kinds of music that were such a large part of Jamar's and Douglas's out-of-school lives. With the boys' demonstrations, guidance, and support, Georgette's "music" gradually became more and more pleasing to her and to her audience.

The children's musical talent came in handy when their literature study groups were invited to create music to accompany the reading of the book being studied. In many ways, this challenge was no different from that facing composers commissioned to write a musical score for a movie. Like writing, making and sharing music constitutes a form of "authoring" or composing.

For children like Jamar and Douglas, whose linguistic power would not soon offer them academic success, there exists the danger that they will lose their faith in themselves as learners, what Smith (1981) calls their "sensitivity." Restoring lost sensitivity is no easy feat; in the process of losing that faith, children often cease taking the risks so critical to effective learning. Essentially, they cease engaging the ideas, the behaviors, and the experiences that would result in academic growth and a feeling of success.

But consider the confidence that Jamar and Douglas have developed through their involvement in a multiage setting and through their success as musicians. Recognized and respected as competent "authors" of musical compositions, an honor earned through their own diligent and focused inquiry, experimentation, and self-evaluation, they have developed an unshakable sensitivity that will serve them well as they approach composing in other more foreign media, and learning in less-familiar disciplines.

The move to cross-aged grouping coupled with broadening the curriculum to include multiple ways of knowing seems a potent combination. By providing several years for teacher and child to uncover what the child knows, and by expanding the ways through which students can demonstrate what they know, we can increase the likelihood that each child will find a way to "connect" with the curriculum, and ensure that all children's voices will be heard. Together, these variables provide a kind of safety net to help guarantee that no child will ever have to fall through the cracks again.

References

BARNES, D. 1992. *From Communication to Curriculum.* 2nd Edition. Portsmouth, NH: Heinemann.

EISNER, E. 1982. *Cognition and Curriculum. A Basis for Deciding What to Teach*. New York: Longman.

GARDNER, H. 1983. *Frames of Mind*. USA: Basic Books.

HARSTE, J. 1993. "Curriculum as Inquiry." *Primary Voices*, 1: 3-7. Urbana, IL: National Council of Teachers of English.

HARSTE, J., WOODWARD, V. AND BURKE, C. 1984. *Language Stories and Literacy Lessons*. Portsmouth, NH: Heinemann.

HUBBARD, R. 1989. *Authors of Pictures, Draftsmen of Words*. Portsmouth, NH: Heinemann.

SMITH, F. 1981. "Demonstrations, Engagements, and Sensitivity. The Choice Between People and Programs." *Language Arts*, 58, 1: 103-112.

WATSON, K. AND YOUNG, B. 1986. "Discourse for Learning in the Classroom." *Language Arts*, 63, 2: 126-133.

WELLS, G. 1986. *The Meaning-Makers: Children Learning Language and Using Language to Learn*. Portsmouth, NH: Heinemann.

WELLS, G. AND CHANG-WELLS, G. 1992. *Constructing Knowledge Together: Classrooms as Centers of Inquiry and Literacy*. Portsmouth, NH: Heinemann.

Creating and Sustaining a Multiage Vision

11

Gary MacDonald

The New Suncook School in Lovell, Maine, is the largest of the elementary schools in MSAD # 72, a small rural school district comprising nine towns in western Maine. As principal of this school, which has a student population of 260 in kindergarten through fifth grade, I am proud of the distinctions the staff has received. They have been honored by The Regional Laboratory for Educational Improvement of the Northeast and Islands for their commitment to establishing a quality learning environment for young children. The school also recently was recognized by *Redbook Magazine* as one of the best elementary schools in the country and is currently featured in a video project entitled *Every Child Can Succeed*, developed by the Agency for Instructional Technology in cooperation with the Council of Chief State School Officers. For the past several years the staff at the New Suncook School has worked to create an environment that supports, facilitates, and encourages critical dialogue about all aspects of schooling. The most significant result of this effort can be observed in the nature of instruction at all levels. Teachers have revised their conception of learning to treat it as an active process of constructing ideas, rather than a passive process of absorbing knowledge.

The program that has brought the most immediate attention to the New Suncook School has been a structural one. Our primary grades are organized into multiage classes, encompassing kindergarten through grade two. Special education students previously assigned to the composite resource room are totally mainstreamed into these classes. Children in the multiage classes remain with the same teacher for three years and have the opportunity to experience continuity from year to year as well as the leadership skills that develop as a result of this structure. Kindergarten students, formerly assigned to either a morning or an afternoon session, now all come to the morning session in order to work with the first and second graders. Our program allows those first-year students (kindergartners) who are ready to stay all day when it is mutually agreed upon by parent and teacher.

The multiage classes allow children to grow and develop at their own pace in an environment that encompasses a wide range of developmental levels. The curriculum is designed to be integrated, meaningful, and relevant to children's lives. Classrooms contain an abundant number of interactive learning centers, and children have many opportunities to choose their learning activities. Through a theme-based curriculum, children incorporate reading, writing, and math skills to explore a theme at their own developmental levels. Instructional practices such as whole language, Math Their Way, the writing process, cooperative learning, and process science facilitate children's explorations. We believe that the students at New Suncook are experiencing an active, integrated learning environment that allows for individual developmental differences and provides opportunities for children to make choices to gain independence in thinking, decision making, and problem solving.

Changes in the instructional practices within the classroom were a catalyst for a re-examination of assessment strategies. Traditional assessment methods, which assumed that all children developed at the same rate, did not take into account children's thinking, decision making, and problem-solving skills. Understandably, because of their own schooling experiences, parents were most comfortable with traditional standardized test information, in addition to the daily dose of "refrigerator-door dittos." We determined that it was critical for us to demonstrate to parents that the students were still being held to high levels of accountability. Through research and discussion the following assessment practices emerged.

- OBSERVATION. Children are observed in whole group, small group, and individual settings. Anecdotal records are kept for each child. Teachers document how students naturally approach learning tasks.
- PORTFOLIOS. Samples of children's work are collected on a regular basis. New Suncook has established a uniform list of the yearly samples that are to be kept in a child's permanent portfolio. This list includes a taped reading conference; a self-portrait; a self-selected journal entry; a cumulative math assessment; a reading log; a research project; and several writing samples.

The structural and instructional changes that have emerged at New Suncook have not been the result of a directive from above nor the result of preconceived notions that certain programs or methods were the only way to meet the needs of young children. In order to understand how we successfully transitioned to and sustained the changes to multiage classrooms, it is necessary to acknowledge the development of a school culture that supported innovation, collaboration, and risk taking.

The success that the New Suncook School has achieved has been due to the extraordinary commitment of the entire staff in a process that began to take root several years ago. In 1985, New Suncook was awarded a small grant entitled "Research Into Practice" (RIP) by the Maine Department of Education. The purpose of the grant was to "provide teachers an opportunity to study and analyze recent educational research and its implementation in the classroom." The success that the RIP team had in building the foundational elements that were critical to the restructuring movement at New Suncook School cannot be overstated. Though met with skepticism at first, the RIP team formed the critical mass that is needed in any change effort. It provided us with an initial structure to explore a collaborative planning model focused on creating learning environments where all students can succeed. In the first year, the emphasis was on "doing what we were doing, better," and so topics such as lesson design, time on task, and questioning techniques were prevalent. After receiving funding for a second year of the RIP team, the focus of our efforts changed from looking at ways to improve our instructional practices to the nature of instruction itself. Asking the question "What are we doing and why?" forced us to begin to examine our basic belief systems about learners, learning, and subject matter.

As a school, we worked to develop a vision statement and a set of shared understandings that would be the basis for our practice. It was critical that we identify and articulate the belief statements that drive our classroom practice. This would insure that as we continued to reflect on practice and develop new learnings, they would be consistent with our stated beliefs. We found that the process of reaching consensus can be a frustrating experience, particularly for those more inclined toward product rather then process.

At the same time that New Suncook was involved in a self-examination of its practices, the district had a recent experience of supporting the creation of developmentally appropriate programs for early learners. The district had adopted the use of Gesell screening for all entering kindergarten students and in the early 1980s had supported a significant training effort in The Early Prevention of School Failure program. The district had supported the creation of an early kindergarten and a transitional first grade in the centrally located town of Fryeburg. Although retaining a firm belief in the philosophical tenets that were driving the district commitment to appropriate programming in the primary grades, the staff at New Suncook began to reflect on how best to provide for primary-age children.

Looking for an alternative to the Early K and T-1 programs first came about as a result of the New Suncook staff's questioning the rationale for placing Lovell students in Fryeburg, and the voiced concerns of parents in the Lovell community. Parents were expressing feelings of guilt because they had failed to teach their children what they needed to know to "pass" the Gesell screening and "make it" in regular kindergarten. Added to this guilt was the knowledge that now their child had to be bused an additional fifteen miles away from the community school on a bus with high school students to attend a special placement class. Parental guilt and concern became difficult to shield from a child, and student feelings of failure began to emerge.

The result of this situation was the development of a proposal by the primary teachers to the school board in the spring of 1988 that would combine kindergarten, first grade, and second grade at New Suncook into a team-taught multiage primary classroom for five- to eight-year-olds. The class was designed to enable children to grow and develop at their own pace in an environment that encompassed a wide range of developmental levels. Children would be able to remain in their neighborhood school, regardless of their developmental level when they entered, and could stay with the same program for three to four years. There would be two years of observation before decisions about extra year placements would need to be made. Primarily for grant writing purposes, the class became known as the MAGIC (Multiage Grouping with Integrated Curriculum) Class. Over the next three years the entire primary unit at New Suncook became multiage classrooms with the former composite resource room students becoming totally integrated into the regular classes.

It is essential to create effective strategies for communicating efforts towards change, and so it was decided to articulate clearly to the community our assumptions about learners and learning upon which the program was built. They are:

1. Children operate on variable biological and psychological time and not on uniform physical time.
2. Each child is unique with his or her own individual patterns of growth, personality, learning style, and family background.
3. All aspects of children's development are integrated—physical, social, emotional, cognitive, and aesthetic.
4. Children's learning is also integrated. They do not distinguish learning by subject area.

5. Primary-aged children learn best through active, rather than passive activities. Learning activities and materials need to be concrete, real, and relevant to the lives of young children.

6. Opportunities to make choices help children gain independence in thinking, decision making, and problem solving.

These six statements, developed in 1988, have served to be the basis upon which many decisions have been made. Similar to the school vision, they are the points of reference that assist in galvanizing the creative efforts of individual teachers. With these statements serving as the backdrop, parents can better understand how the instructional practices that they observe in the classroom can meet the goals of the program.

As the reexamination of belief systems causes classroom practice and school structure, ultimately, to alter, there is a need to seek out and establish avenues for school/community partnerships to help the community understand the changes they see within the school. Parents have expectations and assumptions about school, most of which are based on their own school experience. Realizing that our success was dependent on parents' understanding and, perhaps more importantly, observing their own children's success in our classrooms, we developed several strategies to meet this need.

With the assistance of Dr. Lynne Miller from the Southern Maine Partnership, we developed a project called "Parents and Teachers as Researchers." A group of parents and teachers learned about research design, developed questions about educational practices for individual research, and collected and shared data. The excitement and benefits of parents and teachers sharing data, observations, and findings surpassed any of the participants' expectations. One parent of a multiage student wrote:

> Being involved with this project increased my comfort level with my child's school and its teachers. I think parents often feel isolated from and intimidated by school. By working with the teachers and staff of our school, I gained a sense of familiarity and friendship with individual staff members and confidence in their common educational goals and expectations.

The staff in the primary grades have developed methods of communicating a child's progress to the parents that are much more meaningful and descriptive than had previously been the case. These methods include:

- MAGIC MOMENT BOOKS are specially designated books in which a teacher writes about a proud moment the child has had in school. The child takes the book home and the parent writes about a proud moment the child has had at home and returns it to school.

- THE WEEKLY NEWS is a dictated report by children about daily activities. As the name indicates, it is sent home once a week.

- THE SCHOOL NEWSLETTER contains information about activities in the classrooms and often includes an article about parenting and/or education.

- OF PRIMARY IMPORTANCE is a bi-monthly newsletter sent home to parents. It includes a detailed description of activities occurring in the primary classrooms, upcoming events, and an article about a different curriculum area each issue.

- QUARTERLY PROGRESS REPORTS record a child's progress on a K-2 continuum. This continuum includes the developmental stages of literacy and mathematical growth, which match up with those stages we use when assessing children with our performance-based tools for reading, writing, and math.

- PARENT CONFERENCES occur at least twice a year, or more frequently if requested by a parent or teacher.

In addition to the teacher-initiated activities described above, parents and community members are invited to participate in many other formally planned events that are designed to keep them informed. A significant amount of effort is devoted to building the public's trust in viewing the school's staff as professionals who are using current research, along with their own experiences, to create the best learning environments possible for each individual student.

After several years the New Suncook School has earned a reputation for providing quality classroom programs for children. But that has not come about without significant questioning from the public. It is ironic that although schools are subjected to constant criticism, attempts to substantially transform schools are viewed with such a degree of skepticism that valiant efforts by committed staffs often slowly wither on the vine. In 1990 the school board requested that an evaluation be done of the multiage program. Certainly this request appeared reasonable, except for the fact that no other existing program has been evaluated before or since. After an extensive process involving educators from outside the district, surveys, consultants, staff interviews, and statistical analysis, the conclusion was that "the program has been a successful program." In addition, "the efforts of the staff to create and implement this program were recognized by all to be extensive and commendable." Regardless of the accolades the program has received statewide and nationally, each year the multiage program has to defend itself from elements in the district and community that question its continuation because it looks different in structure or practice.

Our experiences at New Suncook have provided me with several learnings that might be helpful for others who are considering a multiage program to reflect upon. These are:

1. The structure is only important if it enhances the instructional practices. While developmentally appropriate instruction can be enhanced in a multiage classroom, poor instructional practice can be deadly. Therefore, quality staff development experiences need to be continually made available.

2. The entire educational community needs to be involved in creating a vision and supporting belief statements about learners and learning.

3. The creation of a school culture that supports a "norm of inquiry" is essential so that the decisions about programming are not seen as final destinations, but rather as temporary resting points based on the best information at that time.

4. The principal must be viewed as an active endorser and participant in the work of the school.

5. The school needs to create strategies that will demonstrate to the public that quality work is being produced by students.

6. Specialists (physical education, music, art, etc.) need to be involved early in the process of developing multiage classrooms.

7. The support staff (secretary, janitor, bus drivers, etc.) in a school needs to be made aware of the reasons behind the instructional practices, not only for the more obvious reasons, but because they are often a direct link to the community's understanding of what is happening within the school.

8. Change efforts within a school need district-level support. The culture of a school and the resultant changes in practice and structure cannot be sustained in the long term if they exist in a district unaligned with its purposes.

In this chapter I have attempted to convey the necessity of viewing successful change efforts in a school in a systemic way. That is, unless we acknowledge a school as an organizational unit where all parts and players are guided by common visions and beliefs, it will be very difficult to sustain the results of smaller pioneering efforts within the school. School effectiveness is ensured when the community of learners continues to learn about what is effective, how to work together, and what new demands must be met to educate students. Successful programs that have a sustained life within a school do not exist in isolation; they require a school culture that supports the notion of a community of learners in which all parties have skills and insights to offer.

Part Three:
The Research Sphere

Multiage Grouping

Implications for Education

Diane E. McClellan

12

Some years ago as researcher Howard Lane (1947) watched the neighborhood children playing in his back yard, he noted that rivalry, aggression, and lack of compromise were often the order of the day when all the children gathered were of the same age. It didn't matter whether that age was three, or five, or nine. However, when the children who gathered were of varied ages, cooperation and consideration predominated.

Research often begins with just such an observation. The researcher then investigates whether his or her observations or hunches are supported by objective evidence. From such beginnings, a small but growing body of research relevant to multiage classrooms has been conducted. In the following review of the research, I will look at some of the ways that our intuitive hunches or personal experiences related to the benefits of multiage grouped classrooms are supported by research. I will examine possible effects of same-age and multiage classrooms on children's social and cognitive development and argue that increased opportunities for children of disparate ages to socialize and work together deepen and enhance the effectiveness of educational environments and strategies.

The separation of children into same-age groups has become so common in schools and other settings that it is often taken for granted as part of the "natural" order of things. Separation into strict age groups, however, is most often a system of organization imposed by adults rather than by children (Whiting 1963). Ellis, Rogoff, and Cromer (1981) found, upon observing the indoor and outdoor interaction of 436 neighborhood children, that the children could be found in groups of the same age only 6 percent of the time. However, groups consisting of children who differed by at least a year in age from one another were observed 55 percent of the time.

The grouping of children by a narrow age range is in all probability a result of the widespread concentration of large numbers of people into cities through the process of industrialization (Konner 1975). Concurrent with this concentration was the development of what some have referred to as a "factory" model of education, whereby children are grouped in ways that make the delivery of information cost- and time-efficient (Katz 1993). In some ways children are treated as objects that, when subjected to uniform treatment, will yield (at the end of their education) uniform outcomes. This model of education, when followed exclusively, is inconsistent with a wealth of recent research on what happens to the developing human brain (Huttenlocher 1990; Kandel & Hawkins 1992) and the kinds of educational strategies that bring about optimal learning and development.

Nevertheless, a factory model of education, facilitated by single-age grouping, is by far the most common form of classroom organization across the nation. At the same time, children have less access to children of differing ages outside of school than in times past due to: (1) smaller family size, (2) reduced proximity to cousins and other members of the extended family, and (3) a sometimes drastic reduction in opportunity for interaction with other children in neighborhood settings.

"Does this matter?" ask Katz, Evangelou, and Hartman (1990).Urie Bronfenbrenner (1970) suggested more than thirty years ago that it did matter. Bronfenbrenner argued that the United States was rapidly becoming a country segregated by age. Referring to both child-adult and child-child relations, Bronfenbrenner suggested that the segregation of people by ages was at the core of "the breakdown of the socialization process in America" (156). What Bronfenbrenner has pointed to is the much discussed breakdown of community in many parts of the United States. It is possible that many of the hardships children face today, in their families, schools, and neighborhoods, could be dramatically alleviated if schools could find ways to structure themselves to support and nurture, rather than undermine, community—to foster community not just *for* children, but *among* children. Multiage grouping is one such strategy.

Multiage grouping is an educational strategy that has a solid history in American education (Goodlad & Anderson 1959, 1987). The reader is referred to Katz, Evangelou, and Hartman (1990) for the most recent review of the literature. It is also an educational strategy that continues to gather credibility as theory (Piaget 1977; Vygotsky 1978) and educational research (Brown & Palincsar 1989) accumulate on the learning process and its neurological correlates in the development and morphology of the human brain (Huttenlocher 1990; Kandel & Hawkins 1992; Squire 1992). It a strategy that creates one of the necessary conditions for fostering the social, emotional, intellectual, and spiritual growth of children. Multiage grouping is a strategy, in other words, that can help empower schools to do what they were and are intended to do: educate.

Social Development

Same-Age and Mixed-Age Peers Are Both Critical to Social Development

There is increasing evidence that relationships with peers play a central and necessary part in a child's social development and future well being. Children who do not experience adequate social interaction in childhood are at risk for serious difficulties later in life including increased participation in crime, illegitimate pregnancy, depression, and school dropout (see Parker & Asher 1987). Hartup (1983) and others (Goldman 1981) have pointed to the possibility that what is learned socially in multiage groups differs from that learned in same-age groups, and that each type of group contributes to the child's development in unique ways. That is, each may meet a variety of different needs and contribute to the development of different social capacities. Same-age groups, for example, appear to foster the development of playfulness, friendship capacities, and aggression (Whiting & Whiting 1975). Children's exposure to others younger than themselves, on the other hand, elicits greater rates of prosocial behaviors including practice in parenting, caretaking behavior, and altruism (Whiting & Whiting 1975; Lamb 1978; Goodall 1986; Zahn-Waxler, Friedman, & Cummings 1983).

Along with fostering other areas of development, the multiage classroom offers numerous opportunities to support children's social development, including prosocial and friendship behaviors. These behaviors are explored in the next section.

The Importance of the Opportunity to Practice Caring for Others

Prosocial behaviors include helping, sharing, cooperating, and caring for or taking responsibility for another (Radke-Yarrow, Zahn-Waxler, & Chapman 1983). It is commonly and rightly assumed that the quality of nurturing a child receives from his or her primary caregivers significantly influences the development of the child's own capacities for prosocial conduct (Radke-Yarrow, et al. 1983).

The importance of "practice" as a variable in the development of prosocial behaviors such as helping and cooperating has not been examined extensively. However, it is reasonable to expect that prosocial behavior, like most other behaviors, must be practiced to be learned well. If children are given little opportunity to care for others throughout their childhood, it seems unlikely that the dispositions and skills required to respond adequately to the needs of others will magically appear when they reach adulthood.

In *Raising Good Children*, Lickona (1983) suggests that in some respects society has structured out naturally occurring opportunities for children to help one another. Research indicates that this is indeed the case. For example, Radke-Yarrow & Zahn-Waxler (1986) note that attentive staff in preschools frequently step in with their own help before children have an opportunity to help one another.

The Limits of Same-age Grouping

"But can children learn to care for each other just as well with friends and classmates of the *same* age?" teachers and parents question. Yes and no. The evidence does not suggest that same-age mates do not behave prosocially toward one another (McClellan 1991), but it has been demonstrated that older children are more likely to behave nurturingly toward younger children than they are towards their agemates (Whiting & Whiting 1975). This may occur for two reasons. First, the physical appearance or "babyness" of young children is more likely to make older children feel nurturing toward a child younger than themselves (Whiting & Whiting 1975). Second, younger children are more likely to ask older rather than same-age or younger peers for help (Whiting & Whiting 1975; McClellan 1991). This is true for several reasons including that a younger child recognizes that an older child can often more realistically provide the help needed.

Similarly, teachers in multiage classes may be more likely to ask children to help one another than teachers in same-age classrooms. A teacher in a multiage class can genuinely use the help of the five- and six-year-olds in such tasks as trying to get everyone (including the two- and three-year-olds) ready to go outside or down for a nap. There is a good deal an eight-year-old can do that a five-year-old cannot do, whereas a whole classroom of same-age five-year-olds may have less opportunity and ability to help one another. Ridgeway and Lawton (1965) found that younger children in multiage classrooms were noticeably less dependent on the teachers than in the same-age classes where the teacher was the only person of greater maturity.

Decreases in Prosocial Behavior

If children in same-age classrooms have fewer natural and genuine opportunities to behave prosocially, there is evidence that these behaviors do not mature and may even decrease. Knight and Kagan (1977) found that children's behaviors increased in rivalry and decreased in altruism and cooperation as they progressed through elementary school. In a review of published research, Radke-Yarrow, Zahn-Waxler, and Chapman (1983) found that only about half of the studies on altruism show predicted increases in altruism with age. One possible explanation for these unexpected decreases in altruism with age is that current structural factors in many classrooms and in American society tend to reverse biological tendencies toward increased altruism with age. One such structural factor may be the age composition of most American classrooms, the vast majority of which are composed of same-aged children.

The above research showing decreases in altruism can be contrasted with anecdotal (Bronfenbrenner 1970) and empirical findings (Whiting & Whiting 1975) that the capacity for prosocial behavior increases with age in countries where children are given the opportunity and expected to help in the care of younger children. Whiting and Whiting (1975), for example, studied children in six countries including the United States, Africa, and the Philippines. They found that children who were responsible for helping with the care of younger siblings were significantly more altruistic than children who did not have significant responsibility for younger siblings. In a study that is also relevant to this point, Bathurst (1933) found that children who had responsibility for a pet showed more sympathetic responses to other children than children who did not have responsibility for a pet. Children, like adults, gain self-confidence and feelings of self-worth through opportunities to contribute meaningfully to their environment and other people (Katz et al. 1990).

Qualitative Differences in Prosocial Behavior as a Function of Age

Even if a teacher is skilled in helping children of the same age learn to help and care for one another, the quality of the care same-age children provide one another may be of a different nature than prosocial behavior between children of differing ages. Youniss (1980) found that the characteristics of kindness distributed from adult to child, child to child, or child to adult differed from one another. A notable difference was the expectation among children that kindness between children of roughly equivalent age would be reciprocated. The prosocial interaction among age-mates, in other words, is of a more contractual nature—"you scratch my back, I'll scratch yours." While not in any way negating the importance of relationships based on such parity, prosocial behavior among children of differing ages may be closer to that found between adult and child, where "repayment" in kind is not expected. Multiage interaction, in other words, may help children move beyond the contractual stage of moral development (Kohlberg 1968) and prepare them more adequately for future adult roles such as parenting.

The Quality of Childhood Friendships As a Predictor of Adult Behaviors

Researchers have shown that how well a child is liked by other children, or the "sociometric status," is one of the most accurate ways of identifying children who might be at risk for a variety of serious social problems later in their lives (Parker & Asher 1987). There is also evidence that the quality of young children's social competence accurately predicts academic as well as social competence in later grades. The risks in adolescence and adulthood include academic failure, dropping out of school, criminal involvement, and depression (Kupersmidt 1983; Cowen, Pederson, Bibigian, Izzo, & Trost 1973; Parker & Asher 1987).

Some research suggests that children experience greater isolation in same-age than in multiage classrooms (Adams 1953; Zerby 1961). Other research findings suggest that when classrooms are made up of children who are highly similar to one another, there are more social "stars" in the classroom, but also more children who are rejected and/or neglected by their peers (Rosenholtz & Simpson 1984). Thus a few popular children may experience more friendship bids than they can reciprocate, while other children are actively rejected or left out of the loop altogether. McClellan (1991) compared multiage classrooms composed of preschool children with same-age classrooms of preschool children and found similar tendencies.

The children's acceptance by others is vital to their opportunity to learn the kind of social skills that enhance their future capacity to make positive contributions to their personal and professional communities. It is also an important key to cognitive development.

Cooperation, Aggression, and Dominance

Aggression among children, teenagers, and adults is a problem of major and growing proportions in the United States. Although the complete absence of the expression of aggression, particularly playful aggression, in children's relationships is probably not desirable (Pellegrini 1989), research suggests that typical levels of aggression far exceed what is considered optimal (Magid & McKelvey 1987; Zigler et al. 1992). It has been argued that the concentration of same-age peers is a major factor in the extremely high incidence of aggressive, anti-social, and destructive acts in United States society (Bronfenbrenner 1970).

Research tends to support Bronfenbrenner's argument. In an international study, for example, Whiting and Whiting (1975) found that children were more likely to behave aggressively with same-age peers than with peers who differed in age by a year or more. McClellan (1991) compared teacher ratings of aggression levels in seventeen multiage preschool classrooms with those of eighteen same-age preschool classrooms. Findings indicated significantly higher levels of aggression in the same-age classrooms.

Some might speculate, however, that aggression among multiage groups of children could be equal to or even greater than aggression among same-age groups. It might be argued that some older, bigger children would tend to bully younger children. Could the presence of older bullies lead to higher levels of aggression in multiage classrooms? What might account for the lower levels of aggression in the multiage classrooms noted by investigators above?

Studies involving East African children (Whiting & Edwards 1977) distinguish between the distribution of aggressive versus dominant behaviors. Older children did tend to dominate their younger peers, but they were also very nurturing. Dominance, in other words, included nurturance and prosocial behavior. Pure aggression, on the other hand, was seen more frequently among same-age peers in a constellation of behaviors that included rough-and-tumble play, teasing, and insulting.

It is likely that dominance is a behavior pattern that is distinct from, yet related to, aggression (Goodall 1986). One way various animal groups, including humans, allow for the expression of aggressive impulses yet maintain order is through the establishment of dominance hierarchies (Goodall 1986; Maccoby 1980). Established dominance hierarchies serve to reduce the amount of fighting among children because children usually know in advance whom they may safely challenge and whom they had better leave alone (Maccoby 1980). A primary factor in the establishment of hierarchies among adult male primates is age (Goodall 1986). Challenges may be more frequent and stable hierarchies more difficult to maintain if many of the individuals in a social group are too close to the same age, size, and/or physical ability. The process of establishing a dominance hierarchy in a same-age group may be a far more difficult task than in a multiage group, and may thus place a good deal more competitive stress on the group members.

Stright and French (1988) observed the leadership behavior of mixed-age groups of children seven to eleven years old who were given the task of accurately ordering sets of pictures. Older children in the mixed-age groups demonstrated sophisticated leadership capacities by soliciting individual and group preferences and organizing the statements and behaviors of the younger children. The leadership of the older children was skillfully facilitative rather than crudely dominating or bullying. Others have reported similar findings (Graziano, French, Brownell, & Hartup 1976; French, Waas, Stright, and Baker 1986).

The psychological toll for low status in a same-age group may also be greater than in a multiage group. To be low child in the pecking order in a group of five- to seven-year-olds may be at times uncomfortable, but the child knows that in two years his or her place in the hierarchy will change. Children in the same-age class, on the other hand, may be more likely to regard their status as a stable reflection of their worth and acceptance.

There is also evidence that children prefer to be taught by children older than themselves rather than by children their same age, and prefer to teach children younger than themselves (Allen & Feldman 1976; French 1984; McClellan 1991). Again this may be, in part, because older children can more comfortably establish dominance over younger children and, further, because younger children can more comfortably yield to the dominance of an older child without the loss of face that might accompany submission to a same-age peer.

In summary, it has been suggested that the concentration of same-age peer groups in parts of the social fabric of the United States contributes to aggressive and anti-social behavior (Bronfenbrenner 1970; McClellan 1991). One way many animals, including humans, maintain order, is though the establishment of dominance hierarchies (Maccoby 1980). However, dominance hierarchies may be more difficult to maintain if too many of the individuals in a social group are close to the same age and/or ability. Multiage grouping thus may foster leadership among children that is more confident, skilled, and nurturing than leadership efforts exclusively among same-age peers.

Cognitive Development

Multiage grouping is an educational strategy that promotes the development of a fuller range of the child's social skills, which are critical to the child's current and future well being. However, the child's ability to work as a team member, to cooperate with others, to help and take turns with others, and to provide leadership is more than a set of social skills, however beneficial these skills in-and-of themselves might be.

There is evidence to suggest that cognition in higher level mammals, including humans, may have evolved to a significant extent as an evolutionary adaptation to social complexity (Humphrey 1976). Further, there is evidence that the growing child's social interaction is important in the development of his or her cognitive abilities (Tizard 1986). Social cognition may, in other words, lay the foundation for cognition in general within both the development of the individual person and the genetic heritage of the species (Chance & Mead 1953; Humphrey 1976; Jolly 1966; Tizard 1986). If this is the case, we might look at mixed-age groups as providing the child with a rich and complex social environment that contributes to greater social facility, as well as to greater cognitive facility.

Piaget (1977) and, in a more developed form, Vygotsky (1978) have provided a context for understanding cognitive development as being intimately linked to the brain's active construction of knowledge within a social context. Recent findings in neuropsychology on brain development and learning in childhood (Huttenlocher 1990) confirm an organic basis for many of the theories put forth by Piaget and Vygotsky, as well as the educational approaches that have developed in response to these theories. Several central concepts within Piagetian and Vygotskian thought relate to the multiage grouping of children.

Vygotsky: The Zone of Proximal Development

In Vygotsky's (1978) view, the most fruitful experience in a child's education is his or her collaboration with more experienced or skilled partners. Vygotsky's much discussed "zone of proximal development" is that area within which the child (or novice) cannot act alone, but can act in cooperation with a person of greater expertise (see Moll 1990). The "expert" or more experienced social partner provides a structure or an intellectual scaffold (Brown & Palincsar 1989; Bruner 1977), thus allowing the novice to accomplish what he or she may be ready for with support but could not accomplish alone.

Some researchers (Rogoff 1990) have likened this process to a kind of apprenticeship and have suggested that this is the way humans have historically acquired new skills and knowledge. The children in a hunter-gatherer society, for example, learned the skills for adulthood as they actively took part in the work of the tribe; young artists-to-be, rather than enrolling in schools for the arts, learned their crafts as apprentices to mature artisans.

Co-Construction of Knowledge

Relevant to Vygotsky's and Piaget's thinking is a notion discussed by Cairns (1986). Cairns notes that human beings are biologically predisposed to synchronize their responses with those of others. This biological bias toward synchronization, which is reciprocal and bi-directional in character, is supported by overwhelming empirical evidence in animal and human research (Cairns 1986).

A critical feature of apprenticeship is that it is a bi-directional process. It is not simply a matter of the child or novice synchronizing his or her actions and thinking with a person of greater expertise. That scenario is undistinguished from direct instruction or any other instructional technique that systematically leads a child, with human or computer assistance, through a series of steps in a learning process. Rather, central to a Vygotskian perspective, is the process he termed "intersubjectivity," whereby two participants in a task, though starting from different points, arrive at a shared understanding in the course of communication (Tudge 1992). The zone or area of mutual understanding does not exist independently of those who are interacting. Rather it is literally created in the course of their interaction (Tudge 1990).

The need for mutual understanding places a severe constraint on the effectiveness of whole class instruction to foster a child's cognitive development. And yet one teacher cannot be expected to individually and effectively apprentice or mentor twenty-five or thirty children. Other teaching and learning strategies must be found to create the kinds of learning environments consistent with current theoretical and research findings. In multiage grouping, children have many potential mentors in addition to their teacher.

Research Findings for Multiage Classrooms

Empirical findings support the supposition that children's opportunities to interact with more advanced and less advanced peers strengthens their cognitive skills. Behaviors elicited in younger children when relating to peers older than themselves include more mature and cognitively complex play (Goldman 1981; Mounts & Roopnarine 1987; Howes & Farver 1987) and less reliance on adults (Goldman 1981; Ridgeway & Lawton 1965; Reuter & Yunik 1973; Ridgeway & Lawton 1965). Shatz and Gelman (1973), for example, found that the speech of two-year-olds was significantly more complex when they were speaking with four-year-olds than when they were speaking with other two-year-olds.

Mounts and Roopnarine (1987) looked at the play patterns of three- and four-year-old children in same-age versus multiage classrooms. They observed two classrooms of three-year-olds, two classrooms of four-year-olds, and two classrooms of three- and four-year-olds. The researchers found that the age composition of preschool classrooms did affect the social-cognitive play patterns of three-year-olds. In particular, three-year-olds in multiage classrooms were more likely to engage in more complex modes of play than three-year-olds in same-age classrooms. Brownell (1990) also found that pairing older and younger children led to more complex modes of play as the children actively adjusted their behavior to that of others. Further, the older child in the dyads made more complex and frequent social overtures to their younger partners than to their same-age peers.

Piaget: Cognitive Conflict Between Peers as Central to Cognitive Development

Piaget (1977) argues that the most critical resource for the child's advanced cognitive development is interaction with peers. The child's opportunity to argue or debate with peers requires a decentering, a capacity to understand one's own thinking, and, at the same time, the thinking of others. Piaget observes that it is with peers, rather than adults, that the child is most deeply challenged in his or her belief systems. This is because of the more or less equal footing of peers, which frees children to more actively confront both their own ideas as well as the ideas of others.

The drawback to direct instruction, or even less formal interaction with adult teachers, is the tendency for the children to prematurely acquiesce (Brown & Palincsar 1989; Kamii 1973), thus precluding the children's deeper consideration of potential differences in their own views of things and that of their teachers. Ample research (Johnson, Johnson, et al. 1984; Johnson 1991; Ames 1992) demonstrates that children think more, learn more, remember more, take greater pleasure in learning, spend more time on task, and are more productive in classes that emphasize learning in well-implemented cooperative groups than in individualistic or competitive structures. Cooperative groups are not conflict free, however. Rather, consistent with the findings of Piaget, they are places where peers come to deeper understandings by hearing the views of others, expressing their own views, and making cognitive accommodations to synthesize the diversity of opinion.

Piaget and Vygotsky: Relevance to Multiage Grouping

Piaget (1977) makes a convincing case that conflict among children who are not afraid to take on one another is central to advanced levels of cognitive development. However, this does not necessarily lead to the conclusion that classrooms set up exclusively with same-age peers are best at providing opportunities for optimal levels of cognitive conflict between peers. Murry (1982) found that when each child feels he or she has a valid, though different hypothesis from peers, the necessary conditions are present for fruitful intellectual interaction.

In children who are too similar in their thinking there may be little to debate about, little cognitive adjustment that either child needs to make. Shatz and Gelman (1973), looking at verbal communication between children ranging from three to four, found that the closer children were in age, the fewer adjustments the speaker made to the listener. In a related experiment on children's development of moral reasoning, Turiel and Rothman (1972) found that the maximum change in children's reasoning occurred when the arguments that were pitched to them were about one stage higher than their current level of moral reasoning (see Kohlberg 1980, for a discussion of the stages of moral reasoning). Arguments pitched two stages or more above the child's current level of reasoning, as well as arguments pitched to the child's current level, were less effective.

Further, as we have seen, if an entire group of children are too close in age, the competition for dominance may lead to far more social conflict than is optimal for their social or cognitive development. In a related argument, Palmer (1987) argues that the conflict necessary for optimal intellectual development can only occur within a community, so that those interacting will take the time to fully consider one another's position, as well as take the emotional risks necessary for the kind of deep engagement that leads to real intellectual work. Research on the greater teaching effectiveness of those older peers who are intimates to the younger child, such as older siblings (Azmitia & Hesser 1993), reinforces the significance of Palmer's observations about the importance of community to intellectual development.

The increased cooperation and acceptance found in multiage grouping, strengthens the likelihood that a strong and trusting classroom community will develop. In other words, multiage grouping strengthens community, community strengthens trust, and trust strengthens the courage needed to engage in deep debate with others.

It is not likemindedness, then, that leads to maximum cognitive development. Nor are large gaps in age, maturity, or skill levels likely to foster cognitive development. Rather, maximum cognitive development occurs when there is an optimal difference among those in interaction. Further, when a positive social climate is developed in ways suggested by the research already reviewed, the sense of community that develops also promotes cognitive development. Such conditions are consistent with basic tenets to both Piaget's and Vygotsky's thinking. And such conditions are nourished by the multiage classroom.

The Role of the Teacher

While it is beyond the scope of this chapter to discuss the role of the teacher in depth, it is important to be clear that in a multiage classroom, as in any classroom, the role of the teacher is very important. Multiage grouping is one strategy that may facilitate social and cognitive development, but it needs to be used consciously and skillfully by the classroom teacher (Katz et al 1990). Tudge (1990, 1992), for example, found that a child's over-confidence in his or her position could be confounded with expertise. Thus a child who is confident but wrong might lead another less confident child down the wrong road. The teacher must know how to help both children examine and test out their ideas with open minds to settle conflicts. In particular, the teacher needs to model a stance of respect so the younger or less experienced child has the confidence to fully articulate his or her own ideas.

Benefits to Older Children of Multiage Groups

The benefits of multiage grouping to children who are the younger or in-between-aged members of the group seem consistent with an intuitive understanding of the social and cognitive advantages of a mixed-age grouping. However, parents often worry about their child's continued progress as he or she becomes one of the older children in a multiage classroom. Although these fears usually evaporate when parents see a well-implemented multiage classroom, this concern deserves special attention.

Protective and Rehabilitative Effects of Mixed-age Interaction for Older Children.

It is possible that older children who experience social difficulties may be helped by the multiage classroom before formal intervention becomes necessary. Lougee and Graziano (1985) observe that children who are given opportunities to provide leadership for younger children not only assist the teacher in reminding younger students of classroom procedures, but also tend to improve their own behavior.

Furman, Rahe, and Hartup (1979) found that withdrawn children made significant and lasting increases in prosocial behavior when paired with a child several years younger than themselves. Suomi and Harlow (1975) realized similar results with rhesus monkeys who had been isolated from birth and were rehabilitated using normal monkeys three months younger than themselves. The use of the younger monkeys was found to be far superior to any other form of rehabilitation. The dramatic rehabilitative potential of pairing older children with younger ones may also be interpreted as an argument for the importance of mixed-age interaction in preventing serious social dysfunction before it has an opportunity to take root.

Development of Academic, Cognitive, and Leadership Skills

French, Waas, Stright, and Baker (1986), who examined leadership behavior in seven- through eleven-year-old children assigned to mixed- or same-age triads, found that the older group members of mixed-age groups increased their organizational behavior and solicitations of opinion, but exhibited less opinion-giving than their same-age counterparts in homogeneous age groups. Eleven-year-olds in a multiage group were, in other words, more sophisticated and thoughtful in their leadership when they were with younger children, than were eleven-year-olds in same-age groups.

As teachers often have noted, in the process of teaching one also consolidates and deepens one's own understanding. Likewise, children who tutor another child have been found to increase the depth and organization of their own knowledge (Bargh & Shul 1980). Katz et al. (1990) suggest that a similar phenomenon occurs as older children help and instruct younger children in the social conventions of community life.

Conclusion

There are many unanswered questions related to multiage grouping. Just as same-age and mixed-age relationships tend to elicit and reinforce different social and cognitive skills, we might expect that the degree of difference in age between two children would also influence the kinds of skills their interaction reinforces. We might also expect that children at particular ages would be especially likely to evoke particular responses in most social partners. We know, for example, that infants elicit a strong nurturing response from all age groups.

Other questions abound and include the following (Katz et al. 1990): What is the optimum age range for a multiage classroom? What is the best proportion of older to younger children in a classroom? What proportion of time ought to be spent in a multiage setting? What should the curriculum in a multiage setting look like? These and many other questions are intriguing and need further investigation.

Multiage groups usually include same-age peers, with whom skills unique to same-age interaction can be practiced, while same age-groups, by definition, do not include mixed-age peers. The benefits of children's relationships with other children of the same age, then, is assumed to be of great value and is not at issue. Rather, at issue is the disproportionately large amount of time most children spend in same-age groupings and the resulting impact on their social and cognitive development.

Support has been presented for the argument that not only do same-age and multiage interactions develop different social capacities in the child, but that each is indispensable to the child's full social and cognitive development. As formal structures and socializing agents take over what was once an informal network of multiple socializing agents of diverse ages, it is important that we create structures that are capable of eliciting those kinds of social and cognitive skills and dispositions we wish to see our children develop.

No one would argue the importance of protein in the child's diet. And yet few parents willingly feed their children a one-dimensional diet composed exclusively of meat, for example. A variety in nutrients is critical to the health and survival of the physical organism. The research reviewed here suggests that a multidimensional social, emotional, and cognitive environment is no less critical to children's social and intellectual health. Multiage grouping is a key strategy for ensuring that children receive a full range of social and cognitive experience.

References

ADAMS, JOSEPH. 1953. "Achievement and Social Adjustment of Pupils in Combination Classes Enrolling Pupils of More Than One Grade Level." *Journal of Educational Research* 47: 151–155.

ALLEN, VERNON, AND ROBERT FELDMAN. 1976. "Studies on the Role of Tutor." In Vernon Allen, ed., *Children as Tutors*. New York: Academic Press.

AMES, CAROLE. 1992. "Classrooms: Goals, Structures, and Student Motivation." *Journal of Educational Psychology* 84: (3) 261–271.

AZMITIA, MARGARITA, AND JOANNE HESSER. 1993. "Why Siblings Are Important Agents of Cognitive Development: A Comparison of Siblings and Peers." *Child Development* 64: (2) 430–444.

BARGH, JOHN AND Y. SHUL. 1980. "On the Cognitive Benefits of Teaching." *Journal of Educational Psychology* 72: 593–604.

BATHURST, J. E. 1933. "A Study of Sympathy and Resistance (Negativism) Among Children." *Psychological Bulletin* 30: 625–626.

BRONFENBRENNER, URIE. 1970. *Two Worlds of Childhood: U.S. and U.S.S.R.* New York: Pocket Books.

———. 1979. *The Ecology of Human Development: Experiments by Nature and Design*. Cambridge, MA: Harvard University Press.

BROWN, ANN AND ANNEMARIE PALINCSAR. 1989. "Guided, Cooperative Learning and Individual Knowledge Acquisition." In L. Resnick, ed., *Knowing, Learning, and Instruction: Essays in Honor of Robert Glaser*. Hillsdale, NJ: Lawrence Erlbaum Associates.

BROWNELL, CELIA. 1990. "Social Skills in Toddlers: Competencies and Constraints Illustrated by Same-Age and Mixed-Age Interaction." *Child Development* 61: 838–848.

BRUNER, JEROME. 1977. "Early Social Interaction and Language Acquisition." In H.R. Schaffer, ed., *Studies in Mother-Infant Interaction*. London: Academic Press.

CAIRNS, ROBERT. 1986. "A Contemporary Perspective on Social Development." In Phillip Strain, Michael Guralnick, and Hill Walker, eds., *Children's Social Behavior*. New York: Academic Press.

CHANCE, MICHAEL, AND A. P. MEAD. 1953. "Social Behavior and Primate Evolution." *Symposia of the Society for Experimental Biology* 7: 395–439.

COWEN, E., A. PEDERSON, H. BABIGIAN, L. IZZO, AND M. TROST. 1973. "Long-term Follow-up of Early Detected Vulnerable Children." *Journal of Consulting and Clinical Psychology* 20: (5) 797–806.

ELLIS, SHARI, BARBARA ROGOFF, AND CINDY CROMER. 1981. "Age Segregation in Children's Social Interactions." *Developmental Psychology* 17: (4) 399–407.

FRENCH, DORAN. 1984. "Children's Knowledge of the Social Functions of Younger, Older, and Same-age Peers." *Child Development* 55: 1429–1433.

FRENCH, DORAN, GREGORY WAAS, ANNE STRIGHT, AND J. A. BAKER. 1986. "Leadership Asymmetries in Mixed-Age Children's Groups." *Child Development* 57: 1277–1283.

FURMAN, WYNDOL, DONALD RAHE, AND WILLARD HARTUP. 1979. "Rehabilitation of Socially Withdrawn Preschool Children Through Mixed-Age and Same-Age Socialization." *Child Development* 50: 915–922.

GOLDMAN, JANE. 1981. "A Social Participation of Preschool Children in Same-Versus Mixed-Age Groups." *Child Development* 52: 644–650.

GOODALL, JANE. 1986. *The Chimpanzees of Gombe: Patterns of Behavior*. Cambridge, MA: The Belknap Press of Harvard University Press.

GOODLAD, JOHN AND ROBERT ANDERSON. 1959, 1987. *The Non-Graded Elementary School*. New York: Teachers College Press.

GRAZIANO, WILLIAM, DORAN FRENCH, CELIA BROWNELL, AND WILLARD HARTUP. 1976. "Peer Interaction in Same- and Mixed-Age Triads in Relation to Chronological Age and Incentive Condition." *Child Development* 47: 707–717.

HARTUP, WILLARD. 1983. "Peer Relations, 103–196." *Handbook of Child Psychology: Vol. 4. Socialization, Personality, and Social Development*. New York: Wiley.

HOWES, CAROLEE AND JOANN FARVER. 1987. "Social Pretend Play in 2-Year-Olds: Effects of Age of Partner." *Early Childhood Research Quarterly* 2: 305–314.

HUMPHREY, N. 1976. "The Social Function of Intellect." In P .P. Bateson & R. A. Hinde, eds., *Growing Points in Ethology*. 303–317. Cambridge, MA: Cambridge University Press.

HUTTENLOCHER, PETER. 1990. "Morphometric Study of Human Cerebral Cortex Development." *Neuropsychologia* 28: (6) 517–527.

JOLLY, ALISON. 1966. "Lemur Social Behavior and Intelligence." *Science* 153: 501–506.

JOHNSON, DAVID. 1991. *Learning Together and Alone: Cooperative, Competitive, and Individualistic Learning*. Englewood Cliffs, NJ: Prentice Hall.

JOHNSON, DAVID, ROGER JOHNSON, EDYTHE JOHNSON-HOLUBEE, AND PATRICIA ROY. 1984. *Circles of Learning: Cooperation in the Classroom*. USA: Association for Supervision and Curriculum Development Publications.

KAMII, CONSTANCE. 1973. "A Sketch of the Piaget-Derived Preschool Program." In J. L. Frost, ed., *Revisiting Early Childhood Education*. 150–166. New York: Holt, Rinehart, and Winston, Inc.

KANDEL, ERIC AND ROBERT HAWKINS. 1992. "The Biological Basis of Learning and Individuality." *Scientific American* 267: 79–86.

KATZ, LILIAN. 1977. *Talks With Teachers*. Washington, DC: National Association for the Education of Young Children.

———. 1993. "What Can We Learn From Reggio Emilia?" In C. Edwards, L. Gandini, and G. Forman, eds., *The Hundred Languages of Children: The Reggio Emilia Approach to Early Childhood Education*. Norwood, NJ: Ablex Publishing Corporation.

KATZ, LILIAN, DEMETRA EVANGELOU, AND JEANETTE ALLISON HARTMAN. 1990. *The Case for Mixed-Age Grouping in Early Education*. Washington, DC: National Association for the Education of Young Children.

KNIGHT, GEORGE, AND SHARON KAGAN. 1977. "Development of Prosocial and Competitive Behaviors in Anglo-American and Mexican-American Children." *Child Development* 48: 1385–1394.

KOHLBERG, LAWRENCE. 1968. "Early Education: A Cognitive-Developmental View." *Child Development* 39: 1013–1062.

———. 1980. "Kohlberg on Moral Development and Moral Education." In B. Munsey, ed., *Moral Development, Moral Education, and Kohlberg*. Birmingham, AL: Religious Education Press, Inc.

KONNER, MELVIN. 1975. "Relations Among Infants and Juveniles in Comparative Perspective." In M. Lewis and L. A. Rosenblum, eds., *Friendship and Peer Relations*. New York: Wiley.

KUHN, DEANNA. 1972. "Mechanism of Change in the Development of Cognitive Structures." *Child Development* 43: 833–844.

KUPERSMIDT, JANIS. 1983. "Predicting Delinquency and Academic Problems From Childhood Peer Status." Paper presented at the biennial meeting of the Society for Research in Child Development, Detroit, MI.

LAMB, MICHAEL. 1978. "The Development of Sibling Relations in Infancy: A Short-Term Longitudinal Study." *Child Development* 49: 1189–1196.

LANE, HOWARD. 1947. "Moratorium on Grade Grouping." *Educational Leadership* 4: 385–395.

LICKONA, THOMAS. 1983. *Raising Good Children*. Toronto: Bantam Books.

LOUGEE, MICHAEL, AND WILLIAM GRAZIANO. 1985. *Children's Relationships With Non-Agemate Peers*. Unpublished Manuscript.

McCLELLAN, DIANE. 1991. "Children's Social Behavior as Related to Participation in Mixed-Age or Same-Age Groups." (Doctoral Dissertation, University of Illinois at Urbana-Champaign, 1991) Ann Arbor, MI: University Microfilms International Dissertation Information Services.

MACCOBY, ELEANOR. 1980. *Social Development: Psychological Growth and the Parent-Child Relationship*. San Diego: Harcourt Brace Jovanovich.

MAGID, KENNETH, AND CAROLE MCKELVEY. 1987. *High Risk: Children Without a Conscience*. Toronto: Bantam Books.

MOLL, LUIS. 1990. *Vygotsky and Education*. Cambridge, MA: Cambridge University Press.

MOUNTS, NINA, AND JAIPAUL ROOPNARINE. 1987. "The Social Individual Model: Mixed-Age Socialization." In J. L. Roopnarine and E. Johnson, eds., *Approaches to Early Childhood Education*. 143–162. Columbus: Merrill Publishing Company.

MURRY, FRANK. 1982. "Teaching Through Social Conflict." *Contemporary Educational Psychology* 7: (3) 257–271.

PALMER, PARKER. September/October 1987. "Community, Conflict, and Ways of Knowing: Ways to Deepen Our Educational Agenda." *Change*: 20–25.

PARKER, JEFFREY, AND STEVEN ASHER. 1987. "Peer Relations and Later Personal Adjustment: Are Low-Accepted Children at Risk?" *Psychological Bulletin* 102: (3) 357–389.

PELLEGRINI, A. D. 1989. "Elementary School Children's Rough-and-Tumble Play." *Early Childhood Research Quarterly* 4: (2) 245–261.

PIAGET, JEAN. 1977. *The Development of Thought: Equilibration of Cognitive Structures*. New York: Viking.

RADKE-YARROW, MARIAN, AND CAROLYN ZAHN-WAXLER. 1986. "Familial Factors in the Development of Prosocial Behavior." In D. Olweus, J. Block, & M. Radke-Yarrow, eds., *Development of Antisocial and Prosocial Behavior: Research, Theories, and Issues*. Orlando, FL: Academic Press.

RADKE-YARROW, MARIAN, CAROLYN ZAHN-WAXLER, AND MICHAEL CHAPMAN. 1983. "Children's Prosocial Dispositions and Behavior." In P H. Mussen, ed., *Manual of Child Psychology*, 4th ed. New York: Wiley.

REUTER, JEANETTE AND GLADYS YUNIK. 1973. "Social Interaction in Nursery Schools." *Developmental Psychology* 9: (3) 319–325.

RIDGEWAY, LORNA, AND IRENE LAWTON. 1965. *Family Grouping in the Primary School*. New York: Ballantine Books.

ROGOFF, BARBARA. 1990. *Apprenticeship in Thinking: Cognitive Development in Social Context*. New York: Oxford University Press.

ROSENHOLTZ, SUSAN, AND CARL SIMPSON. 1984. "Classroom Organization and Student Stratification." *The Elementary School Journal* 85: (1) 21–37.

SHATZ, MARILYN AND ROCHEL GELMAN. 1973. "The Development of Communication Skills: Modification in the Speech of Young Children as a Function of Listener." *Monographs of the Society for Research in Child Development* 38: 152.

SQUIRE, LARRY. 1992. "Memory, and the Hippocampus: A Synthesis From Findings With Rats, Monkeys, and Humans." *Psychological Review* 99: (2) 195–231.

STRIGHT, ANNE, AND DORAN FRENCH. 1988. "Leadership in Mixed-Age Children's Groups." *International Journal of Behavioral Development* 11: (4) 507–515.

SUOMI, STEPHEN, AND HARRY HARLOW. 1975. "The Role and Reason of Peer Relationships in Rhesus Monkeys." In M. Lewis & L. Rosenbulm, eds., *Friendships and Peer Relations.* 153–186. New York: Wiley.

TIZARD, BARBARA. 1986. "Social Relationships Between Adults and Young Children, and Their Impact on Intellectual Functioning." In Robert Hinde, Anne-Nelly Perret-Clermont, and Joan Stevenson-Hinde, eds., *Social Relationship and Cognitive Development.* Oxford: Clarendon Press.

TUDGE, JONATHAN. 1990. "Vygotsky, the Zone of Proximal Development, and Peer Collaboration: Implications for Classroom Practice." In Luis Moll, ed., *Vygotsky and Education: Instructional Implications and Applications of Sociohistorical Psychology.* 155–172. New York: Cambridge.

———. 1992. "Processes and Consequences of Peer Collaboration: A Vygotskian Analysis" *Child Development* 63: (6) 1364–1379.

TURIEL, ELLIOT, AND GOLDA ROTHMAN. 1972. "The Influence of Reasoning on Behavioral Choices at Different Stages of Moral Development." *Child Development* 43: 741–756.

VYGOTSKY, LEV. 1978. *Mind, Self, and Society.* Chicago: University of Chicago Press.

WHITING, BEATRICE. 1963. *Six Cultures: Studies in Child Rearing.* New York: Wiley.

WHITING, BEATRICE AND CAROLYN EDWARDS. 1977. "The Effect of Age, Sex, and Modernity on the Behavior of Mothers and Children." (Report to the Ford Foundation).

———. 1988. *Children of Different Worlds: The Formation of Social Behavior.* Cambridge, MA: Harvard University Press.

WHITING, BEATRICE AND JOHN WHITING. 1975. *Children of Six Cultures: a Psycho-Cultural Analysis.* Cambridge, MA: Harvard University Press.

YOUNISS, JAMES. 1980. *Parents and Peers in Social Development.* Chicago: University of Chicago Press.

ZAHN-WAXLER, CAROLYN, SARAH FRIEDMAN, AND MARK CUMMINGS. 1983. "Children's Emotions and Behaviors in Response to Infants' Cries." *Child Development* 54: 1522–1528.

ZERBY, JOHN. 1961. "A Comparison of Academic Achievement and Social Adjustment of Primary School Children in the Graded and Ungraded School Programs." (Doctoral Dissertation, Penn State University, 1960). *Dissertation Abstracts International* 21: 2644.

ZIGLER, EDWARD, CARA TAUSSIG, AND KATHRYN BLACK. 1992. "Early Childhood Intervention: A Promising Preventative for Juvenile Delinquency." *American Psychologist* 47: 997–1006.

Conclusion: Full Circle

The mad rush was over; the buses had gone. It was suddenly quiet. As usual, Jane came with a stack of day books to sit at the big worktable in my room. I joined her with a pile of homework papers. "Jane, something great happened today, when you were finishing up the Morning Message lesson."

Jane didn't look up from the day book she was reading. "What was that?"

"It was Dennis. He was sitting right behind Cindy. She had gotten up on her knees, probably to see better, because she's so tiny. Anyway, she was blocking Dennis's view of the chart. Well, he leaned forward and gently tapped Cindy on the shoulder and *whispered* to her, 'Will you please sit on your bottom?' Of course, she sat down, and Dennis was right there, I mean *into* that message, waving his hand to be called on. It was really neat to watch him."

Jane commented, "Well, I guess we *have* come full circle, then. It doesn't seem that long ago that Dennis was the itchy five-year-old getting 'reminders' from the older ones. So many reminders, too! Was he loud! I guess he has grown up a bit."

I considered. "You know, he has. It's great to be able to see these kids change over the years."

Jane closed the day book and looked up. "The kids see changes in themselves, too. I think they are very aware of growing into different roles. First-year students are happy to follow the lead of the big kids."

I put the homework papers aside. "Yes, then in their second year, they are anxious to be helpers and models for the new guys. It's fun to see them begin to realize that they have something to offer. And by their third year, leadership roles seem to come naturally to them."

"It *is* like a circle." Jane paused. "You know, there are many circles in our multiage program. In fact, our day itself is circular. It begins and ends with a circle."

"Have you noticed how the morning stories are almost always about home, and how at the end of the day the children are eager to talk about school?" I glanced at the pile of homework papers and continued, "The children's morning sharing session brings the home to school and the homework brings the school back into the home."

"That's true," Jane commented. She pointed to the bright pumpkin-planting mural on the wall. "The pumpkin project is another way we connect the home and the school. Whole families joined us to help plant the pumpkins a few weeks ago. The pumpkin project is a *year-long* cycle. Each year the new students come into our circle through the pumpkin project."

"And those leaving us often return to help take care of the pumpkins. They don't have to break away from us too abruptly," I added.

"Yeah. Wasn't it good to see Andy the other night at the weeding party? Even though he left us three years ago, now he is back with us because his little sister is part of our class. I'm so glad that Jenny has joined our program."

Picking up the homework papers I tried once again to be productive. "Well, we should get to work."

Jane returned to her day books, but she wasn't quiet for long. "You know, sometimes connections go back a long way. Think about our work. Twenty years ago we were teaching together in a multiage program. Now we're back at it again!"

"Don't you think we teach a lot differently now than we did then, though?"

"In what way?" Jane asked.

"I think that we focus more on our own learning now, as we are planning our teaching. We figure out what has been meaningful to us as learners, and what strategies we use. We recycle our own experiences. We have found that what works for us works for children, too."

"Yes, like the process of creating portfolios. And writing in our day books. And working collaboratively," Jane added.

I thought for a moment. "The children stimulate our learning, too. I've learned a lot about how to ask questions from the kids. There is a circle of continuous learning that goes back and forth between us and the children."

"A much larger circle of learning is the connection we make with all the people we have met who are interested in multiage. Think of all the visitors we've had," Jane said earnestly. "We've learned as much from them as they've learned from us."

"I like what you said earlier about coming full circle. But it doesn't stop now with Dennis and Cindy. The multiage circle will keep expanding."

Jane agreed. "Of course it will. It will keep growing as we continue to reenvision multiage education."

"Whew, all this philosophical talk is too much for me at this time of day," I complained. "Don't you think it's time to go home?"

Jane laughed. "But I was just warming up. I haven't even gotten up on my soapbox yet. I've got at least another hour's worth! Seriously though, it is getting late. We can continue this discussion another time."

Carrying our book bags, we walked together to our cars.

Appendices

Message Checklist Week of: NAME	Actively listens—	Suggests meaningful words—	Attempts sound spelling—	Supplies standard spelling—	Contributes to message discussion—

Parent Survey

Name: _____ Date: _____

I am happy about:

_____

I am concerned about:

_____

I want to know more about:

January 10

Dear Parents,

The ten baby hamsters are all doing well. They are starting to leave the nest and Louie spends all her time running after them to put them back where they belong. We guess motherhood is the same for animals as it is for us! So far six of the babies have been spoken for and will leave us in two or three more weeks. We still have four adorable hamsters looking for adoptive parents. If you are interested in taking on this responsibility, please send us a note. Soon!

We are continuing our study of the book *The Boxcar Children*. We will be sending home copies of the book's illustrations to help your child retell the story to you as we read the chapters. We will be reading the book on Tuesdays, Wednesdays, and Thursdays at Investigations Time. Two major themes of *The Boxcar Children* are independence and problem solving. We'll concentrate on these areas in the activities that we do in the next few weeks. Among other things, this week's investigations will focus on measurement as we discover the size of a boxcar and how it relates to the size of things in our classrooms.

There were several questions on the parent survey about our math program. We base our math program on the *Curriculum and Evaluation Standards for School Mathematics* published by the National Council of Teachers of Mathematics. This book, which was published in March of 1989, has become the guideline for teachers nationwide. We feel it is a common sense approach to math that emphasizes understanding math concepts through the use of manipulatives before using pencil and paper computation. It is our belief that an understanding of math concepts is essential to the development of a love of mathematical problem solving. Our hope is that our students will become life-long mathematicians, as well as life-long readers and writers. We are enclosing the overview of the section of the Curriculum Standards for grades K-4. We know it is lengthy, but we hope you will take the time to read it. If you have further questions about our math program, please call us.

Sincerely,

Penny and Jane

Possibilities for End-of-the-Day Questions

What did you do today to help yourself become a better reader?

What did you do today to help yourself become a better writer?

What good thinking did you do in math today?

What did you do today to help someone else?

What did someone do to help *you* today?

What was the most interesting thing you learned today?

What work did you do today that you value?

What was the best idea you had today?

What did you do today that was taking a risk?

What good thinking did you do today?

How did you cooperate with someone today?

What good talking did you do today?

How did you show someone that you cared for him or her today?

How did you follow our philosophy "Treat others the way you would like to be treated" today?

What work did you do today that you are proud of?

What will you tell your family this evening about your school day?

Communications Workshop Goals

Name _____ Date _____

Today's Date _____ Date of Goal Review _____

Goal #1

Goal #2

Goal #3

Goal #4

APPENDIX F

··

MAINE SCHOOL ADMINISTRATIVE DISTRICT # 49

Multiage Classroom
Progress Report—Primary Level

Student's Name _____

Teacher's Name _____

School _____ Year _____

Assigned to _____ for the _____ year

Days absent _____ Times tardy _____

Assessment of student progress in the multiage classrooms is an integral part of the total program. Assessment is carried out continuously within the classroom by both the students and the teachers to help us know what we have done and what we should do. Assessment helps our students see their progress towards becoming educated people. Assessment helps teachers reflect on our teaching and see the relationship between our actions and student learning. Assessment helps parents to be aware of the priorities and goals within our classrooms.

This checklist is an attempt to give parents a knowledge of their child's learning achievements, strengths, and educational needs. It is a communication tool. It is our hope that strong communication between parents, students, and teachers will be a major part of the multiage program.

KEY

NA = not applicable—child has not yet worked on this topic.

EFFORT:

1 = consistently tries

2 = tries most of the time

3 = tries with encouragement

4 = puts forth little effort

ACHIEVEMENT:

Students will develop at different rates through the following reading and math stages. There is normally a correlation between the time children spend in the program and their progress through the stages. We expect that by the end of three years your child will have moved through the three stages and be operating consistently at the highest level.

READING STAGES:

Emergent Reader—a student at the earliest stage of reading—just beginning to see the connection between oral language and print. Enjoys being read to.

Early Reader—recognizes some sound/letter relationships and is able to use them to read and to write.

Independent Reader—chooses varied reading materials and reads different books for different purposes. Shows confidence in his/her reading. Understands what s/he reads.

MATH STAGES:

Concrete—works with manipulatives to solve problems.

Semi-abstract—uses pencil and paper as well as manipulatives.

Abstract—is able to understand math concepts without the use of manipulatives.

	NOV.	JAN.	APRIL	JUNE
PERSONAL AND SOCIAL GROWTH				
Expresses positive self-image				
Is growing in knowledge of consequences of personal actions				
Complies with school rules				
Works cooperatively				
Plays well with others				
Demonstrates sensitivity to the feelings of others				
Participates in group decision-making tasks				
Respects material and works of others				
Initiates own learning				
Makes responsible choices				
Seeks help when appropriate				

	NOV.	JAN.	APRIL	JUNE
Cleans up after working				
SPECIAL CLASSES Physical Education				
Art				
Music				
THEMES Shares ideas and materials on themes				
Applies overall knowledge and experiences in theme work				
LITERACY DEVELOPMENT **READING** Stages: emergent, early reader, independent reader				
Reads for information				
Reads for pleasure				
Selects a variety of books				
Participates actively in literature groups				
Reacts to stories				
Makes connections between stories				
Reads with understanding				

	NOV.	JAN.	APRIL	JUNE
WRITING				
Finds topics easily				
Writes about personally meaningful subjects				
Develops sense of story				
Is developing effective vocabulary				
Is willing to revise				
Edits own work				
Is developing capitalization				
Is developing punctuation				
Forms and spaces letters and words legibly				
SPELLING				
Uses temporary spelling				
Correctly spells common words				
Recognizes spelling errors				
LISTENING, OBSERVING, AND SPEAKING				
Demonstrates critical listening skills				
Listens courteously				
Uses observations for thinking and expressing				

	NOV.	JAN.	APRIL	JUNE
Communicates effectively orally				
MATHEMATICS Stages: concrete, semi-abstract, abstract				
Applies numbers in practical situations				
Counts objects correctly				
Understands mathematical concepts of:				
Addition				
Subtraction				
Multiplication				
Division				
Computation:				
Addition				
Subtraction				
Multiplication				
Division				
Uses appropriate mathematical symbols				
Is developing problem-solving skills				

	NOV.	JAN.	APRIL	JUNE
Understands fractions				
Estimates and works with measurement				
Is building concepts of time				
Counts money				
Recognizes and names geometric shapes				
Surveys and graphs results				
Records results of mathematical observations				
SOCIAL STUDIES AND SCIENCE Demonstrates curiosity and asks questions				
Observes and recognizes relationships in the environment				
Is developing beginning research skills				
Shows growth in using scientific procedures				

Conference Notes

Parent's name _____   Student's name _____

Teacher's name _____   Date _____

_____

Student comments:

_____

Parent comments:

_____

Teacher comments: